EXPERIENCES OF ABORTION

EXPERIENCES OF ABORTION

DENISE WINN

An OPTIMA book

© Denise Winn 1988

First published in 1988 by
Macdonald Optima, a division of
Macdonald & Co. (Publishers) Ltd

A member of Maxwell Pergamon Publishing Corporation plc

British Library Cataloguing in Publication Data

Winn, Denise
    Experiences of abortion.
    1. Abortion — Personal observations —
    Collections
    I. Title
    363.4′6′0922

    ISBN 0-356-14140-3

Macdonald & Co. (Publishers) Ltd
3rd Floor
Greater London House
Hampstead Road
London NW1 7QX

Typeset in Century Schoolbook by
Leaper & Gard Ltd, Bristol, England

Printed and bound in Great Britain
by The Guernsey Press Co. Ltd., Guernsey, Channel Islands.

CONTENTS

INTRODUCTION

This book is about the emotional aspects and consequences of abortion, not about the practicalities of how to acquire one or about the politics of abortion itself.

Abortion is essentially an emotive subject which arouses strong feelings, for or against. Even so, it is still not an easy subject to talk about for those who are personally involved, loaded as it is with social and personal blame and shame, and with ill-founded assumptions about the ease with which it is undertaken.

Few women undergo an abortion lightly, and there are many who *don't* believe in abortion in principle but suddenly find the alternative intolerable in practice. Even when the decision is, or feels, both right and necessary, it is still one that may bring much pain and conflict in its making, and a whole range of feelings in its wake — sadness, guilt, anger, confusion, grief.

Many women believe that, because they have 'chosen' abortion, they have forfeited their right to soft feelings such as sadness or strong ones such as anger. They suppress these normal reactions which may resurface many years later in unexpected forms, not apparently connected with abortion, and which may affect the whole quality and content of their lives.

A hypnotherapist who works with women who cannot conceive told me he has often found that unexpressed grief about an abortion was working as a psychological block, preventing conception. When, under hypnosis, the feelings were released, such women were able to say goodbye to the baby they had lost and to become pregnant again very soon afterwards. The power of the subconscious can be strong indeed.

This books aims to be one small step in removing the taboo that surrounds abortion. By setting down the emotional experiences of a number of women who have had abortions, and by adding the perspective of two abortion counsellors, it aims to show that a whole range of feelings, often conflicting, are both natural and normal. I hope that by sharing the experiences of others, women who have not dared to speak about their own abortions will give themselves 'permission' to have their own feelings, whatever these turn out to be, and will find someone understanding to talk to, if they have the need.

There is no attempt here to generalise. Individuals do not only react according to their circumstances in life, but according to their personal pasts, their beliefs, their fantasies, their character make-up. Women who have abortions because they are single and at a crucial stage in their careers do not all act one way, while women who have abortions after having children do not all act in another.

I found the 12 women featured in this book (their names have been changed) with the help of various organisations and through word of mouth. Some were in their teens when they had an abortion, some were aged around 40. Some were single and childless, others married with children. Some knew they could not cope with a child, some had partners who did not want the baby. Some suffered failures of contraception, others failed to use contraception. A few had repeat abortions. Two terminated their pregnancies after prenatal diagnosis of foetal abnormality.

They are not intended to stand as being representative of 'the experience' of abortion. They were not randomly selected, in the statistical sense, and are not a cross-section of society. They speak as individuals. But, between them, they have experienced a very wide range of emotions about and after abortion and, I am sure, several parts of many different women's experiences will strike chords for others, regardless of differing backgrounds, education or economic circumstances.

In most cases, I approached *them*. They did not seek me out. I wanted to find women who were not necessarily impelled by the particular horror or pain of their own experience to talk about it, but women who were willing to share, as a way of helping others, whatever their own experience happened to have been. They are not all regretful, although some are. They did not all experience conflict before making their decisions nor did they all find difficulty coming to terms with their choice. A few did not feel that abortion has significantly affected their lives.

The women speak very much for themselves. In Chapter 1 they describe their circumstances at the time of discovering pregnancy and recall their immediate feelings. Chapter 2 looks at those whom they told about their pregnancy, particularly partners, how the news was received, and the impact of its reception. Chapter 3 describes their experiences of professional 'help', or lack of it, from doctors and counsellors, in the making of their decisions. Chapter 4 explores the experience of abortion itself. In Chapter 5, the most lengthy, they describe the feelings abortion aroused in them, immediately and then later, and the effect it may have had on their lives. Chapter 6 looks at the value of personal support after abortion, particularly, where applicable, post-abortion counselling or groups.

It becomes clear from their stories that sympathetic counselling, at the right stage, can be — or could have been — enormously useful in helping women to address fully the variety of emotional issues involved and to come to terms with their decision. In Chapter 7, two very experienced and sympathetic psychotherapists/abortion counsellors share their wisdom on the subject. Chapter 8 provides some useful addresses for more information or help.

I wish to make a few final and context-setting points. Firstly, I have not tried to cover the experience of abortion that arises from rape, which seems to me to require completely separate treatment as one, enormously traumatic, issue.

Secondly, although the women featured in this book were all able to have abortions, the decision is ultimately, in this country, not that of the woman but of two doctors, a decision made on medical or social grounds. Despite the belief of some that we virtually do have abortion on demand, that is far from being the case. In a telling letter to the magazine *General Practitioner*, Diane Munday, public relations officer for the British Pregnancy Advisory Service quoted, as an example of this, the case of a woman of 22, divorced with two children. She had suffered a miscarriage five months earlier and was pregnant again after her ex-husband forced her to have sex while he was drunk. She was refused an abortion by a National Health Service (NHS) consultant.

Finally, this book does not take a position on the rightness or wrongness of abortion, although I personally believe women should have the right to choose. It takes as its stance that abortion is rarely a painless decision and a woman may need help to heal. I hope it will be helpful to many women and I am immensely grateful to psychotherapists Gillian Isaacs Hemmings and Mira Dana and, most especially, to the 12 women who so fully shared their own, often very painful, memories and experiences with me.

1.
DISCOVERING
Reactions to unplanned pregnancy

Discovering that you are pregnant when that pregnancy is not planned is inevitably frightening. The future changes in an instant. Something irrevocable has happened, whether the pregnancy continues or not. It is a time of enormous conflict for most women, whose reactions may be simultaneously positive and negative. Even for those whose initial *thought* is that they do not want to bring a child into the world, because of circumstances of their own, the initial *feeling* may be excitement, pride and satisfaction. They may be shocked, frightened and confused by such conflicting thoughts and feelings.

Surprisingly, it may become clear to many women in retrospect that the conflict predated the moment of discovering pregnancy; that some deep and unrecognised conflict in the way they were trying to live their lives actually led to their becoming pregnant in the first place. Becoming pregnant can be about more than having babies, as two psychotherapists explain in Chapter 7.

Two years on, Joanne is one who feels that there was more to her falling pregnant than pure accident, although she had no idea of that kind at the time. She was 22, had been with her boyfriend Ben for two years, and her life had become chaotic. She had started a job in London as a copytaker on a newspaper, which often entailed shift-work. She commuted between London, where she stayed at her parents' home, and Sussex, where she stayed in Ben's flat.

'Ben was a bit put out when I got the job in London, as I had been working locally till then,' she said. 'He would have been upset if I had got a place of my own in London, as it would have signalled we were moving apart. I didn't really know what was going on with me, in that respect, then, so I stuck with commuting.'

She discovered she was pregnant during a week's holiday with Ben in a cottage in Derbyshire.

'My period was already late when we got there. But it was often late and I had, in fact, very often had to do pregnancy tests because of that. Doing them was traumatic but the results had always been negative.

'I was so confident this time that, yet again, it was a false alarm that I went to the chemists and bought both a pregnancy testing kit and a packet of condoms! When the test was positive, I simply couldn't believe it. I kept asking myself, why this time? Now, I can trace it back to Ben's birthday when we both got rather drunk and we didn't have any condoms.

'I was shocked. I felt confused and terrible and yet I wanted to feel excited about it. I felt different about myself at once when I knew I *could* have a baby. I instantly got into the feeling of being pregnant.

'Later, after the abortion, I went on a post-abortion therapy course and we were asked if we could think why really we might have got pregnant when we did. I thought and thought and felt more and more sure that, for me, having a baby was symbolic of having a home.

'I had really wanted to move to London, rather than remain a displaced person commuting between my parents' home and Ben's home. But I hadn't consciously faced that need to feel settled and I didn't have much money either. A friend of mine had been given a housing association flat when she got pregnant. It must have all connected up for me, unfortunately in this way. My first need was for a home, not a baby.'

Sarah, a 38-year-old solicitor, could also see, in retrospect, that her life was undergoing a frightening upheaval during the year that she twice became pregnant and had an abortion.

She was living with her boyfriend John, 12 years ago, when her father died. Her father had been a very powerful, threatening figure in her life and exerted much influence over her.

'It was an extraordinary time,' she said. 'I had had long hair since I was a child because my father had never let me cut it. Suddenly, at 26, I decided to cut it, very much in defiance of my father. I was saying, "I'm going to live my own life" and I wrote and told him. He was in America at the time. Five days after posting the letter, before he had received it, I got a call saying he had died.

'I remember saying to John, after he died, that we could have babies now. John had never been accepted by my father because he wasn't Jewish. After the funeral, I discovered I was pregnant, so I must have been pregnant before he died.

'It was all so extraordinary. Momentous events one after the other. A whole scenario of life and death. I felt it wasn't happening to me. I felt completely out of control, as if I were going round on a wheel. Death and life and death.'

She knows, at a practical level, how the pregnancy happened. 'I had always wanted children,' she said. 'I had been on the contraceptive pill but had lost interest in sex and we had heard that it was possible that the pill diminished libido. So I came off it. (I now think my loss of interest was more to do with the state of our relationship.)

'I had also always felt that the pill takes away the relationship between having sex and having babies. You don't have to negotiate anything when you are on the pill. When you are using the diaphragm, you have to think "shall I or shan't I use it?", knowing the consequences. But there's no need for that kind of constant awareness of the consequences of sex when you take the pill.

'When I stopped the pill, I was taught to use the diaphragm by a battleaxe of a woman at a family planning clinic. I couldn't understand what I was supposed to be feeling for, to be sure I had inserted it right. Finally I felt so stupid that I pretended I had understood.

'I also had an idea in my mind that, if I did have an "accident", it might inform me how I *really* felt about having a baby. I felt that, because the relationship between the pill and babies had been so remote, how could I truly know what I felt about them?

'I think I knew that the diaphragm wasn't in right because I could feel it moving during sex. But it didn't stop me. When I discovered I was pregnant, I was very thrilled in an instinctive kind of way. However, I didn't know whose baby it was, as John and I had what we saw as an open relationship at that time and I had another friend who was sometimes a lover.'

'The baby did and didn't feel precious. I remember I was careful crossing roads, that sort of thing, and yet it didn't feel so precious that I had to hold on to it. It wasn't a great wrench to consider losing it — I considered abortion as soon as I discovered I was pregnant. And yet I can remember a pleasure that I had this baby inside it. I was very out of touch with my feelings.'

Claire, a 33-year-old secretary, feels she too was out of touch with her feelings about herself and her life when she became accidently pregnant, 14 years ago, at the age of 19. And she too had had a difficult time when she had tried to get contraception.

'I was at college and not very happy. I had started a serious relationship with another student, Anthony, and I went to a clinic for contraception. They made me feel as if I was a naughty girl, so I went away and didn't use anything. I just had this blind faith that I wouldn't get pregnant. Although I was very attached to Anthony, we certainly hadn't planned permanency.

'I can remember nothing about how I actually felt on discovering I was pregnant. I had cut off from it, I think. I only knew I didn't want a child. It is only now, after years of therapy, that I imagine I was too unconnected with myself to have any real feelings about it. I felt guilty about having any feelings at that time, felt I didn't have any right to complain about or demand anything. Any feelings

I did have would have been suppressed.'

Grace, wise and self-questioning now aged 53, feels sad when she recalls how blind and trusting and ignorant she had been at 19 when she fell pregnant. She is American and was living in South Carolina, where she was born.

'The boy was my second boyfriend and my period was never late. I remember, for that while, waking up in the morning and feeling good because it was a new day, then experiencing a leaden weight when I remembered that my period hadn't arrived. I felt worried but not extremely worried. I hadn't had any extreme shocks yet in my life. Young people believe in miracles.

'And yet some part of me knew. I had pains in my gut and my doctor prodded and said it was my appendix. I found myself saying, "I wonder if I might be pregnant too", although I really didn't imagine I could be. So he did the test.

'When it was positive, I wasn't terribly bothered. My family knew my boyfriend and his family. They approved of him. I just assumed we would get married.'

Gillian, also 19 when she became pregnant, was typical of very many teenagers in her reaction. She denied the truth to herself as long as she could. 'I was in my second year at college and my boyfriend Rob was a librarian there. I didn't find out till I was three months' pregnant although deep down I must have known. I had never been late with a period. But I just wasn't in touch with myself.

'I was actually feeling sick, couldn't walk around much and was quite depressed — probably because of what I was blocking out. It was when I could no longer get into my jeans that I finally had to face the truth.

'When I went to the clinic Rob came with me. The sample was negative. But I knew it was wrong and they told me to see the doctor anyway. The doctor was heavily pregnant herself. She said, "Yes, you are pregnant. Now what are you going to do?" I wanted to go away and think.

'I had terrible dreams about chopping people up. But I also felt proud I could be pregnant. I wanted to tell everyone and wear maternity dresses. But it was an awareness of pregnancy rather than awareness of a baby, although I liked the idea that there was a baby there.'

She too felt there were explanations for her pregnancy beyond the obvious. 'I must have known I could get pregnant. I had tried the contraceptive pill but stopped because my mother told me it was dangerous. She never suggested an alternative, though. It made me realise afterwards how much influence my mother had on me.

'She had always said to me, "Don't have children. Look at me with five. Don't get married. Have a career." I think I took all that on without thinking about it. I thought my mother was perfect then. But I was unhappy.

'I had these ideals, from her, about being strong and independent. I was living alone and I was lonely, but I said I loved it. I didn't see that much of Rob because he lived on the other side of town, and I had the fleeting thought that I'd get more attention if I were pregnant.

'Subconsciously I think I did it to get attention. Or because I felt a baby would love me. I have only thought all this out since. At the time I took no responsibility whatsoever for my getting pregnant.'

Catherine was in very different circumstances. At 35 and in a relationship with a man she loved, she knew she wanted a baby. However, the nature of the relationship was not clear-cut.

'We had been together before and parted and had, by that time, been back together for six months. We were serious, in that we felt a lot for each other, but we only met at weekends because I was living and working in London while Nick was in Manchester. We were living completely different lives and hadn't got a clue how to get it together. I had landed a job as an arts administrator which I adored. He was in upheaval, having just sold his business, but he hated London.

'We went on a holiday in Scotland and were very much in love for that whole time. He was talking about our opening a bed and breakfast place there together. It was semi-serious but scary.

'I was using the diaphragm but sometimes, during the

safest part of the month, I didn't put it in. When we got back from Scotland, I didn't use it and I think I was tempting fate. I was going as near as I dared and, I feel, in the depths of myself, I wanted to take the risk. I also wondered if I *could* get pregnant. I was 35.

'When I failed to have a period, I was nervous and excited. When the pregnancy kit I bought showed positive I felt both "Yes! I want a child!" and "Oh dear, maybe not", because Nick and I hadn't sorted anything out about how we were living our lives. I thought about the pregnancy only as a joint thing, not me having a child on my own.'

Maria, a graphic artist, was a year younger, 34, when she discovered she was pregnant. She had been told by doctors she was probably infertile. 'An endocrinologist who tested me for hormonal abnormalities when I went 11 months without a period said I probably only ovulated once every two years, if that. But because of that risk I would still have to use contraception. So I grudgingly used the diaphragm.

'Then I met Stuart. He was the first person I had ever felt really totally in love with. I had never ever wanted children in my life but I felt a rush of desire to have a child with him. I had been a bit off and on about using the diaphragm by the time I met him, as nothing ever seemed to happen. With him, I didn't bother with it at all. But this was before I had the feeling of wanting his child. When he discovered I wasn't using anything, he went wild. His previous partner had also been told she was infertile and she had got pregnant. When they split up it had been a huge wrench for him to leave his daughter.

'I assured him it was all right. Looking back, I had no right to. But I remember, on our first idyllic holiday together, *he* said to me one night, "Let's go and make twins". It was our joke, but only half a joke, that we would like twins. And I remember really hoping it would happen.

'I honestly believe that being so in love and letting myself for the first time entertain the thought of children set my hormones back on track. I think my "infertility" was largely psychological. I started having very regular periods and, although I didn't get pregnant on the holiday, two months later I did.

'When I was two weeks' late, I decided I had better have a test. I really, at that time, didn't think I could be pregnant but I was aware of a slightly alarming soreness of the breasts. It so happened that a friend of mine was the matron of a clinic that did mainly abortions. She said she could do a test for me. I was definitely hoping that it would be negative because, despite my positive emotional response to the idea of having a baby with Stuart, the thinking part of me didn't want that at all. Not then, not so soon, not unplanned.

'When she rang and said, "I'm really sorry to have to tell you this . . ." I remember my stomach dropping through the floor. I whispered, "Shit, no" and had to rush urgently to the loo. I just sat there, my head spinning, my mind incapable of holding on to any one thought long enough to get me into any state of acknowledgement or preparation. I was terrified, particularly as Stuart and I had been together for only seven months and because I had been so insistent that I couldn't get pregnant.'

Diana had already had three children and was 41 when she fell pregnant for the fourth time. She had custody of her two young teenage sons from her first marriage and her third son, William, by her present husband, was not yet two.

'I was 39 when Will was born. For myself, I wouldn't have chosen to have another child but I knew Len desperately wanted a child of his own. Part of me was thrilled for us to have one together but another part of me was ambivalent. I didn't have the same energy at 39. I became depressed for a while because I was obliged to keep on working (Len is an actor and his earnings are erratic). But I didn't like having to leave the baby. I also needed to be sure my other two didn't feel left out. It was a hard time, juggling everything.

'Then, a year later, I experienced the severe shock of being made redundant. I was a picture researcher for a book publishers and I had worked there so long, it was a bit like getting divorced. I had to set myself up as a freelance and that was very nerve-wracking. I was just getting sorted out when I found I was pregnant again. I felt as if I'd sink beneath the waves if I had another child.

'I'd had a false alarm a little while before and thought to myself, "You aren't taking enough care with the diaphragm". And then I started getting lax with it again. It was rapidly obvious to me when I became pregnant.

'I shouldn't have had these diaphragm failures and I feel, in fact, that something was going on. I had had an abortion before, when my first marriage was going wrong and I had a passionate affair with a lover that also ended. I was disturbed by the end of the affair and by the mess of my marriage, and the pregnancy was like a cry for help.

'Perhaps the second one was a cry for help too. It was a year of a lot of change. Len had had a pretty serious, if brief, affair which we openly discussed and sorted out. But I think I was still frightened of losing him. I was unsure whether he loved me and yet, here I was, with a young child limiting my own life in all sorts of ways. I certainly didn't get pregnant to tie him to me. It was more a histrionic thing, a way of saying "Help! Look at me!"'

Joyce, a manageress of a shoe shop, also considered her family complete when, at 39, she fell pregnant. But she feels very much a victim of circumstance. She had a 19-year-old son whom, since he was two, she had brought up as a single parent. Three years ago she married for the second time. Her husband is nine years younger.

'Richard was convinced he didn't ever want children or I never would have married him. I had enjoyed being a mother but I didn't want to give up another 20 years of my life. We agreed I should be sterilised and the operation was done two years ago. In fact, I had tried to get sterilised many years before but the hospital always refused to do it.

'I was five months' pregnant before I knew it. I had always been irregular with periods, so that was nothing to worry about. But when it went on, I did have a pregnancy test just to be on the safe side, and it was negative. A second one a month later was negative too. I didn't have any conclusive symptoms of pregnancy. My breasts were sore but I suffer from mastitis. I was thickening a bit around the waist but thought it was age. When you have been sterilised, you just don't keep thinking you are pregnant.

'Then I went to see my gynaecologist because I had a cyst on the vagina. He was the very same man who had performed my sterilisation. He examined me and said gently: "I don't like to do this to you but I think you are pregnant." I just burst into tears and said, "Please don't make me have it!"'

'I was in panic and shock. Psychologically I had counted out pregnancy. And yet a tiny part of me was relieved because I now knew why something had felt wrong.

'I knew I didn't want the child. I knew it must be quite big. But my emotions were all mixed up with the turmoil and I just didn't feel very much as if I had an actual baby inside me.'

Andrea did. 'I knew instantly I was pregnant and I just couldn't bear it,' she said. 'I felt as if I had a disease. It wasn't like having life inside me. It was like something evil and yet the evil had nothing to do with the father.'

Her own strong reaction surprised her because she wanted children so much and she does now have a young son, whom she chose to bear as a single parent.

'I had always wanted children. I remember, when we were young, my sister used to say she wanted to be an air hostess and I'd say I wanted children. I remember, too, saying to my mother, "If I ever get married, I'll love my children more than my husband." She was shocked.'

Andrea discovered she was pregnant for the first time in the autumn of the year that she was 32. She was a self-employed training consultant at the time and travelled a lot in her job. An important and intense relationship with someone she had known for years kept ending and then starting again but, at that point, she hadn't seen him for about 10 months.

'There was another man, an American whom I had known for years — and still do. He was lovely, rich, attractive. We used to sleep together sometimes when I was over there. I can't remember what I was doing about contraception at this time. I think I had recently come off the pill.

'When I got back to England, I felt a bit odd. I felt tired as if from a hangover. My breasts got sore. Then my period didn't come. I just couldn't believe it. A week later I went to my doctor and my fears were confirmed.

'Because I wanted a child so badly, I felt I shouldn't have reacted so negatively towards being pregnant. I just felt so dirty. I don't know why I felt like that, because the man's so nice! But it was a very, very strong feeling. I knew what I was going to do. There were no doubts or question marks in my mind.

'Perhaps, for all my desire for children, it was just too early. Perhaps I wasn't yet ready to settle down and be a single parent. I've never ever told the father about any of it.'

Three women had second pregnancies and second abortions, and felt very differently the second time.Gillian, the student who had denied her first pregnancy till after three months, couldn't believe she was pregnant again but, once accepted, her feelings were akin to Andrea's.

She was still with her boyfriend, Rob, but only saw him at holiday times because, by then, a year later, she was studying abroad. 'I had become nervous about sex and I wasn't sure about Rob anymore. We didn't actually have full sex, that was the point. It seemed such a non-event that I wouldn't even have remembered it if I hadn't got pregnant. I still can't quite piece it together at all and I still feel bad about it.

'I had some good feelings the first time but the second time there was nothing but bad feelings. I felt the presence as evil the second time. I felt so angry and hard done by.'

Sarah, whose father had died at the time of her first pregnancy, had had an intra-uterine device (IUD) inserted after her first abortion. The first abortion had been in the spring. By autumn, when her relationship with John was breaking up, she found she was pregnant again.

'I felt so angry and cheated by contraception. I felt I had done everything right this time. Why should I have to go through it all again? My body felt cowlike. Big and heavy. I didn't enjoy the experience, the feelings, at all, not like the first time.

'Looking back all these years later, I think I was so arrogant. I had no humility towards how things turned out. There was my body, defying all forms of contraception, and I just thought, "I'll have a baby when it is convenient for me, in a relationship I want, where I can be supported. *I* shall be the one to choose."'

Claire's second pregnancy came three years later, when she was 22. She had been deterred from using contraception by the critical attitude she felt at the family planning clinic when she was 19. By this time she and Anthony had married and Claire was using the pill.

'We had been on holiday in Europe. I got diarrhoea from a tummy bug and I suppose that is when the pill failed. I remember sitting on a bus after visiting my parents and being sick into a plastic bag. That's when I knew.

'I felt sheer terror and panic. We were both still at college and the plan was, when I finished that year, that I would get a job to support us while Anthony took a higher degree. He wasn't eligible for a grant and we were struggling along on mine, with help from my family. If I had a baby, then he wouldn't be able to study.

'I think I did want that baby, in my heart of hearts, but again I suppressed all my own feelings. Anthony was so obsessed with his education and he depended on my support. Really I desperately wanted *him* to be supportive, to be an adult, a man, and prove me wrong.'

For two women, the decision whether to continue a pregnancy only arose because they were discovered to be carrying abnormal babies. Anna, a Cypriot, is 32 and now has a healthy four-year-old daughter. But she has had three late-stage abortions because she and her husband both carry the thalassaemia trait, relatively common amongst Cypriots.

The trait itself has no effect on either of their own lives. However, because they both carry it, any child of theirs has a one in four chance of being born with thalassaemia major, a disease of the blood which requires monthly blood transfusions for life. Until the advent of a drug called Desferal, children with thalassaemia major developed complications from a build-up of iron and rarely lived beyond their teens. The drug eliminates the iron. However, it has to be injected, by syringe pump, for 12 hours almost every day and there may still be complications with other organs in the body.

During her first pregnancy seven years ago, Anna was advised to have a fetoscopy which, if done between 18 and 20 weeks, can show whether the baby is affected. It takes one week minimum for results to be available and often much longer. In keeping with common hospital practice under such circumstances, parents are rung with the results as soon as they are available, day or night. Anna received her call in the early evening.

'It was like an explosion when we knew it was positive. We knew the possibility was high and, yet, we hadn't really known much about thalassaemia and didn't really think it would affect us.

'The doctor who rang was very friendly and sympathetic. He said a bed was available if we wanted to terminate. My husband, thank goodness, was with me when he phoned. We had thought beforehand that, if the test was positive, we would terminate, but when it comes to the crunch, it's not so easy to go ahead just like that. We just couldn't say, there and then over the telephone, "Yes we'll come in". We were heartbroken and in a state of shock, because we just really didn't believe it would be a bad result.

'It is such a late stage, 20 weeks. You are just starting to feel well, you are feeling the baby growing and people are starting to notice and ask when it's due. The pregnancy is common knowledge.

'At that stage, therefore, it was extremely difficult to decide what to do, knowing, too, that we had to decide quickly. I didn't then understand fully what thalassaemia major was, but I had heard enough to frighten me.

'All I could do was cry. It was a case of convincing ourselves to keep to our original decision. But it had to be my husband who phoned the hospital back a few hours later, to arrange the hospital bed. I couldn't go near that phone. I just couldn't stop crying.'

Joan, now 37, had already had the tragic experience of caring for a handicapped child and seeing him die at the age of six. Her first child, born when she was 28, had a rare enzyme disorder called Hunter's Syndrome. It is a sex-linked genetic abnormality. Males suffer it and females carry it. Hunter children have a very short lifespan and, on average, die by the age of eight. Joan's son was mentally retarded, never spoke and was never continent. One day he caught an infection, wasted away and was dead by the end of the month.

Joan has a healthy son, now five. But in 1986 she became pregnant for a third time. 'I went into the pregnancy not quite sure if that was what we wanted. We felt more than anything that we owed it to our son for him not to be an only child,' she said.

She had a diagnostic test, chorion villus sampling (CVS), which can be done at eight or nine weeks but which isn't always conclusive. 'The doctor had a bit of difficulty getting a sample because it seemed I had a fibroid which I hadn't known about. But the lab technician was satisfied they had enough.

'I heard the results just after Christmas. The baby was a girl, so all would be fine, because only boys can have Hunter's. I was thrilled.

'Then came a call from the hospital to say they were a bit concerned. They weren't sure the baby really was a female because it was quite likely that they were maternal, not foetal, cells in the sample. I would have to have an amniocentesis after all (a diagnostic test which cannot be done before 16 weeks).

'I was very anxious during the next 10 weeks, before I could have the amnio. I was also trying to keep a bit detached from my pregnancy, trying not to get involved with the baby because of the risk. It made it easier that way, I felt, to accept a termination if necessary.

'I did have the amnio and the baby turned out to be suffering another condition altogether. Turner's — a rare chromosome deficiency which only affects girls. I was carrying a girl and she had the most severe form of Turner's. The children have no ovaries or breasts. They are very short, have webbing of the neck and kidney problems, amongst other things.

'Most abort spontaneously. Yet I'd had both CVS and amniocentesis, both of which carry a risk of miscarriage, and I still had the baby.

'We were told over the phone late one evening and were absolutely devastated. The doctor said they were 99 per cent sure of their diagnosis but I ought to have a fetoscopy to check, the results of which would take a week. She explained it all and said I could phone her back, apologising for having had to tell me over the phone.

'I cried. Steven had just come in and we talked straightaway and decided there was no point going through the additional strain of a fetoscopy. Having had one severely handicapped child, I couldn't ever bear to go through it again. It was so horrific that both syndromes were so rare and yet it had happened to me twice.'

2.
TELLING
The response of those who matter

The reactions of partners, families or close friends to the news of an unplanned pregnancy inevitably help shape a woman's own feelings towards it, strengthening her resolve to have or not to have a child. In the time of turmoil, between discovering a pregnancy and deciding whether to continue it in difficult circumstances, those who have supportive partners are lucky indeed. But when partners are accusing, or abdicate responsibility, the inner conflict for the woman is much magnified.

If there is someone in the woman's life who is sympathetic and non-judgemental and who will listen and guide as she explores her conflict, the decision, whatever it is, is obviously easier to reach and bear.

However, many women do not dare to speak of their pregnancy to anyone, either because of the fear, or perhaps the knowledge, that those close to them would not understand, and/or because of social taboos. A woman who is contemplating abortion commonly feels immense guilt and self-blame, regardless of whether those crosses should be hers to carry.

By the very nature of the fact that they talked to me, the women I interviewed were not among those who dared not speak of abortion. Only one, Andrea, told no one of her abortion either at the time, or for many years after, but that was her conscious and deliberate choice.

Andrea, the training consultant, had always strongly wanted children but not necessarily a live-in partner.

When she became accidentally pregnant by a friend, hers was the unexpectedly strong reaction that she had evil inside her.

'I knew I was going to arrange an abortion as quickly as possible,' she said. 'I didn't tell anyone, not even the father. If I had talked about it, it would have made the pregnancy more real.

'It didn't even occur to me to tell my sister — we are very close. I felt no shame or regret. I just felt dirty and I couldn't wait to get it all over with. The specialist tried to dissuade me but I was deaf to all he said.' Andrea acted so speedily that the foetus was only five weeks old when she did have her abortion.

Only one other woman remembers not talking about her feelings to anyone close but she, in contrast, would dearly have liked the chance. Grace, now 53, who became pregnant in South Carolina when she was 19, felt very much the victim of the conventions of her society, exacerbated by the fact that she was too young and inexperienced at the time to know her wants and needs.

She had expected, when she found she was pregnant, that her boyfriend would marry her.

'I told him what had happened and he said, "Gosh, what do you want to do?" I asked him what _he_ wanted to do and he said he needed to think. He wasn't antagonistic in any way. The next thing I knew, he had lit out of town.

'I was stunned. I was totally dazed and I remained dazed throughout after that. I told my doctor that he had gone and he was unbelievably shocked. He knew my family very well (I was living away from home) and he knew the boy's family. He said I would have to have an abortion because I shouldn't spoil my life at this stage. But abortion was illegal. He didn't know how to go about finding me one but told me to leave the matter to him.'

Grace had initially gone to her doctor because of appendicitis. Two nights later her appendix blew up and she was admitted to hospital as an emergency. Because she was under-age, her parents had to be phoned for permission to operate.

'My mother came to see me and I told her I was pregnant. She was shocked but got excited at the thought of a lovely wedding — she wouldn't believe that the boy had left permanently. When it did become clear that he wasn't coming back, she became instantly practical about abortion. (The doctor had got a "lead" by then.) She was a very conventional middle-class Southern American. But a child out of wedlock was for her an even worse prospect than an illegal abortion.

'No one ever enquired whether I wanted that child. I didn't know what I wanted but I was never led to think about it or to talk about my feelings. I was dazed by the pregnancy, by the surgery for my appendix and by the boy leaving. I just followed the path down which my mother and the doctor were leading me.'

All the other women I spoke to were able to tell their partners about the pregnancy, but some felt let down by their partners' response. Of those, some were able to confide in and draw support from family or friends, others felt very much alone with a double dilemma.

Joanne, who at 22 had been commuting between her job in London and her boyfriend Ben's flat in Sussex, felt shocked and hurt by the fact that Ben, 24, refused to discuss or fully acknowledge her conflicting feelings about being pregnant. She had found out while they were on a week's holiday in a cottage in Derbyshire.

'As soon as I told him I was pregnant, he said I would have to have an abortion because he was too young to be a father. I was feeling both terrified and excited about the pregnancy, but he didn't want to talk about it in any way that made it feel possible for me to have the baby.

'He tried to act normally for our last two days, as if nothing had happened, because he couldn't see any point in spoiling the holiday when there was nothing we could do till we got back. I just put my head in the sand. I was happier in this limbo than having to make a definite choice not to have the baby.

'Ben didn't want anyone to know about it and he didn't want me to tell anyone either, although I think he knew I would. I wanted to tell people to see if they responded with "how exciting" or "how awful". I was trying to find my way. I knew a single mother, for instance, and I wanted to talk to her. But I didn't want to tell my mum. Only if I decided on having the baby.

'I knew I was storing all this up till I got home and could phone people. Meanwhile, we stayed in the cottage and it was very odd. Such a big thing had happened and we weren't even talking. Ben was a Catholic and I was the first girl he had ever slept with. I think he felt what had happened was because he had sinned.

'I felt resentful of the fact that he hadn't even told his parents we were living together. Now I felt even more resentful because, in the circumstances, a baby was specially unthinkable for him.

'I think if he had felt happier, I could have felt happier about being pregnant. I hadn't actually felt unhappy about it in the first place. But the two days of negative vibes from Ben got to me and I felt increasingly distressed.'

By the time Joanne did talk to her friends, she was starting to feel very negative about her pregnancy.

Sarah, whose pregnancies occurred during a time of great personal confusion in life, the first shortly following her father's death, had an 'open relationship' with her live-in-lover John. It is not the way she would choose to live her life now.

'I told him at once. I remember sitting on his knee and both of us saying we shouldn't have the baby because we didn't know whether it was his. I had wanted to keep it. But I couldn't have taken that feeling very seriously because I went along with it when John said he didn't want the baby. I rang the other possible father and told him what was happening and he didn't object.

'My mother wanted me to keep the baby. But I didn't feel in any great conflict at all — even though I wrote in my diary that, though I was having an abortion, I felt very loving and caring and protective towards the baby. I didn't understand or act properly on my feelings at that time in my life.' Both 'fathers' and her mother remained very supportive, before and after the abortion.

'But my relationship with John went downhill after that,' she said. 'I don't know if it was because of the abortion or my father's death. We never got the spark back. I wasn't conscious of resentment towards him but I realise, in retrospect, that I did feel resentful of him for not holding on to me more and helping me accept what life had sent me.'

When she became pregnant again several months later, as a result of an IUD failure, she had already told John that she planned to leave him. This time there was no doubt that John was the father.

'John was about to leave for Scotland, on work, when I discovered I was pregnant. He was angry with me because I had wanted to leave him. I told him on the phone and he just said, "tough" and left me to it.

'I felt he was justified at the time because, if I had been staying, we would have kept the baby. But he never *tried* to make me stay. Now I think he was foul to me. He wasn't in England at any point over the abortion. My mother took care of me.'

Both Joanne and Sarah had felt an instinctive pleasure and surge of positive feeling about being pregnant; but also an ambivalence, the negative part of which was reinforced by their partners. Catherine, 35 at the time of her pregnancy and keen to have a child, felt no ambivalence on her own part. But her partner's reaction was all important to her. He was still living in Manchester and she was in London, so their time together was restricted to weekends.

'I went to Manchester feeling very nervous about telling Nick. He met me off the train and I told him at once, I couldn't keep it in. I was watching for his reaction and I saw no pleasure, just shock. I felt very disappointed. I realised it wouldn't be plain sailing. We went for a stiff drink.

'We talked and he kept saying, "It's the wrong time". He felt financially insecure because he had just sold his business and was doing a bit of this and a bit of that. In fact, he could have scrapped the lot and come to London, but he had never wanted to live there.

'I argued. There was my age to take into account. It was hardly the time to end a pregnancy, because it mightn't happen again. It felt a bit special to me that it had happened at all.

'I had the idea that I could stay in London, working right up till the last minute and having the baby there, while he sorted himself out, and then I could move up and join him.

'He didn't like that. He said it wouldn't suit me to give up my job, as an arts administrator, because I loved it so much. In retrospect, I think he just couldn't make the commitment. He was terrified and didn't want the responsibility for me and a child. Fair enough, he did have a lot on his plate. And he liked me paying my own way.

'At the end of that weekend we hadn't reached a decision. It was awful. I had to come back to London not knowing what would happen. I did go to see a doctor, but I wasn't in any way ready to make a decision yet.

'Nick never really put his cards on the table. He didn't say, "have an abortion" nor "have the baby". At one point he did say, "I suppose we had better get married" but I couldn't say yes to that because he didn't really *want* to.

'Three friends knew and my two sisters. They were super and supportive but I don't think they could be objective enough to be able to help me.

'Most of my conflict was that Nick wouldn't come clean. It went on over two or three weekends. One weekend it seemed as if it was going to be all right. He went and talked to the one male friend he rated highly. I sat and waited in the garden and thought that, whatever this friend advised, Nick would do.

'The friend advised that we should go ahead. It would be a whole new life. I was over the moon! Then, the next weekend, I was talking about plans and he looked at me and said, "I didn't say I'd have it". It was a bolt out of the blue. That's when I decided on abortion.'

For Claire, planning to support Anthony financially while he studied for a higher degree, the age-old dilemma of 'not the right time' featured very strongly in decisions about her second pregnancy. But, as perhaps for Nick, the argument about time disguised a deeper concern.

Claire had had a first abortion at 19, through which Anthony had been supportive. 'It brought us closer. We had told no one else and we were like two frightened children. It was then that we talked about marriage. I wasn't sure at first but eventually agreed.

'At that stage, I didn't want children and didn't know if I ever would. I was 22 the second time I got pregnant. Anthony's place at college was terribly important to both of us. I had virtually ignored my studies and put my energies into looking after him. But there was no way he could take up his place if I had the baby.

'I told him and he left it up to me but I knew he didn't want a child. I didn't feel supported. Part of me knew that I would be dumped at some stage if I went ahead. I felt he couldn't sustain a relationship that included a child.

'I talked to a girl at college. She was a bit shocked and surprised. I had needed to talk to someone else other than Anthony but I don't think she was the right person. She couldn't take it in or understand.

'I had been quite depressed at times in my youth. I now went down a big black hole. I didn't know myself at all. I tried to live up to others' expectations of me all the time and I was falling very short. I couldn't cope with my failure.

'Anthony and I talked but neither of us was able to talk fully. I can't really remember much about that part. I recall his fear most of all. He was frightened that he might not get what he wanted, that I might not have an abortion. He left the choice with me but I certainly felt the responsibility of it.

'In the end I had to handle it all myself. But that was the nature of our relationship anyway.'

Very many women, some of whose stories are recorded here and others I spoke to in the course of research, made similar points about responsibility. Partners were often resented if they did what they thought was the fair thing and left the choice up to the woman. Even if the woman truly felt that she would be supported whatever she did, she still experienced a sense of burden at having to make such an important decision effectively alone.

Gillian in particular felt enormous resentment that her partner, who was indeed supportive, not only left the choices to her but was not obliged to go through the medical procedures she had to face. She was 19 and still at college.

'When I went to the clinic for a pregnancy test, Rob came too,' she said. 'But he had to wait outside. I remember wishing he could have come in, so that he too would have to answer some of the nasty questions I was being asked.

'Afterwards, while I was thinking about what to do, I felt very angry and I thought I was angry with Rob. I felt it was absolutely outrageous that I, and not he, was the one who had to get out of the scrape we had both got into. He was very under pressure at the time, with work, so I had to do all the practical things and make the phone calls.

'I felt so cross that there was no role he could play. I know it sounds daft but I really wanted *him* to have to have a medical examination and everything that I had. I pushed him away a lot then because he couldn't share equally what I was going through.

'I think I also felt angry at the situation and felt helpless because, to get out of it, *I* had to make a decision. I had never made a decision in my life. When Rob said he would go along with whatever I wanted, my instant thought was, "Oh no!"

'At one stage he said that, if we had the baby, we would have to stay together and did we know each other well enough (we had been together for nine months) to be sure that was what we wanted? I took that to mean that he would leave me, though he didn't mean it that way.'

Like Claire, Gillian also told a woman friend but felt afterwards that she too had chosen the wrong person. 'She was a new friend,' she said, 'and I think I expected a lot more support from her than I got. She was glad that I had confided in her and, as if in return, she told me that she had been raped a few years back. That was so momentous that I had to ask her about it, but it wasn't what I wanted to be talking about at that stage. I needed someone who would give the attention to *me*. Instead we discussed the rape and my feelings were forgotten.'

She did, however, discover support in two unlikely quarters and valued the unexpected help she received enormously. A male friend whom she knew was against abortion turned out to be very sympathetic and non-judgemental when facing someone who was experiencing the dilemma of decision in reality. As Rob lived quite some distance away and Gillian spent a lot of time alone in her rented room, this friend took it upon himself to visit frequently and make sure she was not too depressed.

The other help she received was even less expected. Gillian, although not a Catholic, was attending a Catholic college.

'My tutor demanded to know why my essay was late and I broke down and burst into tears. He was wonderfully supportive, even though he himself was Catholic. He said he would lend me the money for a private abortion if that was what I decided I wanted, and he gave me his home telephone number to call if I needed to talk. He was about 60 and he was just wonderful. He still keeps in touch.'

Gillian's mother was the one who had strongly impressed upon her daughter that it was better to have a career than to marry and be tied down with children. Gillian had taken on her values and attempted to be strong and independent without questioning what she herself wanted.

She said: 'I told my mother by letter the day before the abortion. She phoned and said how awful it all was. But we both found it difficult to talk about feelings and so there wasn't much real contact even then. I hadn't wanted her to be involved before but I had got upset while waiting for the abortion date and suddenly wanted to share with her what was happening. I resented for a long time afterwards that she hadn't got more involved then.'

The two women who already had children both felt completely supported by their husbands. Both women were themselves 100 per cent clear that they didn't want another child. They knew the decision they wanted to make and were quite willing, after discussion, to be responsible for that decision.

Diana, who had two children from her first marriage and a third, then aged two, in her second marriage, had thought instantly that she would have to have an abortion. She was 41, struggling to cope with a new job and a toddler as well as two early adolescent boys.

'Obviously I discussed it with Len. I remember him saying it was the wrong time for a baby, because William was an absolutely exhausting child. (He used to get up six to eight times a night until he started school. It was like medieval sleep torture.) I was aware, however, that Len didn't say he would *never* want another child. He is three years younger than I am.'

Len himself said: 'It was difficult for me because I *did* want more children but I recognised that it would be hard to cope. It was like experiencing a woman's right to choose at the hard end but I respect that. It is just that, knowing we won't have another child (Diana is now 44) has been a bleak and bitter pill to swallow.'

Joyce, who has a 19-year-old son and was sterilised after she married for a second time, said: 'I was in turmoil from the point of view that I don't agree with abortion yet I felt abortion was the right decision for me. Richard agreed. I don't like doing away with any form of life but our focus was on the quality of life a child would have. I still feel there would have been resentment from me against that child if I had had it.

'Both of us think generations do make a difference. I would have been an older mum. Richard, of course, is only 30 but he himself had resented the fact that his own mother was much older.

'The GP had said why didn't we have it adopted. But I

couldn't have had a child and then given it away. We both felt that was terribly unfair on a child.

'I did worry that, despite the fact Richard had not wanted children, he might regret later that he would never be a dad. But I had to let *him* make that decision. I threw so many questions at him to get to all his feelings. I said that if he strongly wanted the child he must say so. Had he done so, we would have had a difficult situation and I would have gone back with him for proper counselling, even though time was against us.' Joyce, because she had been sterilised and so felt protected from pregnancy, and because two tests had been negative, was already over five months' into her pregnancy when it was finally confirmed.

She talked to two or three friends as well as to Richard. 'Mainly I was looking for reassurance that I wasn't being unreasonably selfish. They all supported me. We didn't tell Richard's parents. They couldn't have coped. I have not been in touch with my own mother for years.

'I didn't tell my son either. I felt it was too much to ask him to understand. He and his girlfriend are planning on getting a place together and are looking forward to having children of their own. I think it would have sparked off too many emotions.

'However, he resented the fact that Richard knew why I was going into hospital but he didn't. So I told him it was a fibroid that I had and then he was okay. Afterwards he told me that he had feared I had breast cancer.

'It was unfair of me to have left him so long without any explanation. We worry about our children but tend not to want to bother them when anything is the matter with ourselves. They are so selfish at that age, you don't expect it to be important to them. I was wrong.'

Joan and Anna, who were both at risk of having abnormal babies had agreed, with their husbands, to choose abortion should that turn out to be the case. Joan had steeled herself for the eventuality, keeping herself psychologically slightly detached from her pregnancy. Anna had not expected a bad result from prenatal testing and she and her husband Paul were devastated.

Anna, though she had enormous support from Paul, felt, like many other women, the awesome burden of responsibility was hers alone. 'I feel I carried the bulk of the decision-making. Paul felt that we ought to terminate but stressed that it was up to me. It made me feel totally responsible and I wasn't too grateful for that at the time. I think, in the long-run, however joint the decision may seem, it is always the woman who ends up responsible, I'm afraid.'

Maria feels extremely grateful that there were a number of important people in her life who helped her, at every stage of a traumatic and turbulent month, to explore her anxieties, and who offered unqualified support. She also feels that her partner, Stuart, who, like herself veered between positive and negative feelings, did *not* opt out of the final responsibility. Her memory of that time is clear and supported by a detailed diary.

Maria had for years believed herself infertile. Then when she met Stuart and experienced, for the first time, a positive desire for a baby, she began to think she *would* be able to get pregnant. When it actually happened, however, it was a frightening shock.

'Judy, the friend who happened to be a matron at an abortion clinic, gave me the results of my pregnancy test over the phone. I was shaking and disbelieving. She was marvellously practical and matter of fact. She said she would be home by 7pm and I should call round and we would talk through how I felt and what I should do.

'She made me write out two lists, pros and cons, and said she didn't think my cons were terribly convincing. When I looked at them, they didn't seem so enormous to me either. But the biggest was the fact that Stuart and I had been together only seven months and he already had a child, from whom he was parted, by a woman he had lived with who had also thought herself infertile. I was terrified of his anger. I felt it would be justified.

'I was having weekly therapy sessions at the time, started as an aid when I was trying to give up smoking (I failed) but then carried on for its own sake, as I had really

started to uncover important things about myself. I
considered keeping the pregnancy a secret until I had seen
Sally, my therapist. Or perhaps even having a secret
abortion. Then I strongly felt, no, I had to be honest and
honourable and see Stuart that night.

'I just went over to his flat at 9.30pm, not knowing if he
was in. He wasn't, but he came back half an hour later. I
said I had to talk to him but I couldn't get a word out for
ages. He asked if there was someone else. And then I told
him. There was a long silence. Then he said: "What shall
we call her?"

'My heart just leapt in warmth and gratitude to hear
him say that. We held each other but I told him that I
expected no firm decisions now and that if he changed his
mind there would be no recriminations. No abortion, he
said. If I had an abortion, that would be the end of us.

'I saw Sally the next day and my pride and excitement,
which I hadn't allowed myself to feel till then, came out.
Stuart came round that night and said he had found
himself singing at work. He said perhaps we ought to
consider getting married. Considering we were both
terrified of marriage, that really felt like he was making a
real commitment.

'The next day, though, I met some friends who had
children. They started getting excited for me and talking
about babies and suddenly I felt confused and resistant, as
if I didn't want to join this club. I was starting to feel tired
and, because I had suddenly had to give up smoking and
drinking, I was getting irritable and depressed and not
enjoying much.

'We had agreed we must start looking for a flat together.
I owned mine, Stuart rented his and didn't have much
capital. I started getting anxious, especially as everywhere
was expensive and my work (I was a home-based graphic
artist) was suffering with all the time lost looking. I felt I
was doing more of that than Stuart. I also kept feeling,
"Do I really want any of this?"

'I remember of this time that some days were idyllic
and many were miserable. Stuart had given up smoking in

support, so he was irritable too, and he was anxious about money as he had only just gone self-employed. One night he got drunk and said on the phone perhaps I should have an abortion. I was stunned, especially knowing what abortion meant to him.

'The next day he didn't even remember saying it and was so apologetic, saying there was no part of him that did want an abortion. I was grateful for my sessions with Sally then because she got me to see how hurt and frightened I felt by what he had said, even though, superficially, I had accepted his apologies.

'I told Stuart all that and we both felt better and got our old magic back, but it didn't last. I got terribly depressed. In therapy it came out that I still felt hurt. And frightened that he might go off and leave me with the baby. There was nothing he could do to prove he would stay and that felt bad. Like nothing could be completely right again.

'I started secretly to wish I could have a miscarriage. I saw women with prams and felt daunted. I don't remember whether I had any more good feelings about the baby at all. I was a drag. I remember one night complaining to Stuart that it felt as if my life had come to a stop and that I just felt under stress, about flats and everything. He said the stresses would get much worse than this and yet already we were getting worlds apart.

'The next night he rang me at 1am. He had been drinking. He just said, "Do you *really* want the baby?" and I found I couldn't say either yes or no. He kept repeating the question. It was terrible. I asked him to come down.

'He sat on the bed and said he had searched his feelings and found far more fear about having the baby at this time than he had realised. He didn't think he could go through with it. And that he had never ever heard me say I really wanted the baby.

'I was shocked. For all my negative feelings and wish for a miscarriage, I had never thought again about abortion. I asked, "What about us?" and he said, "I expect it's the beginning of the end".

'I was in floods of tears. We lay apart in bed and it was a terrible night for both of us. I felt I was losing everything. But in the morning he pulled me to him and held me and said that, for all his feelings about abortion, our love was stronger. We were losing our love in our panic over the baby and he wanted to save it. We agreed I would have an abortion *for* us, not against us. I think I felt an enormous relief. But that wasn't the end of it for either of us.'

Maria felt grateful that, even though she had good friends who knew of her anxieties and tried to support her, she was able to benefit from the more objective help a therapist could give. Other women too felt, in retrospect, that they could have benefited from counselling. Those who had unsupportive or frightened, and therefore unhelpful, partners often felt as alone with their awesome dilemma as if they had told no one at all.

3.
DECIDING
The contribution of professionals

The decision to ask for an abortion is rarely instant, automatic and painfree. Only one of the women I spoke to, Andrea, decided immediately, told no one, required no counselling aid, and to her memory, had no anxiety about her decision.

'I would have gone crazy if I couldn't have had an abortion. I feel it would have wrecked my life,' she says. 'The feeling that I had something evil inside me, not life, was so strong. That is what made me know it wasn't right, because I actually wanted children so much.'

Some of the others knew instinctively that they didn't want, or couldn't cope with, a child but they did not choose abortion without mixed feelings. One or two were against the whole idea in principle but, when faced with the reality of an unplanned pregnancy, could make no other decision that was personally right for them. Some of those who might have been expected to greet the chance to end pregnancy with nothing but relief, in fact felt enormous conflict.

As shown in the previous chapter, the reactions of partners, close family and friends have a strong impact on what a woman decides to do. But fewer than half of those I spoke to ever received aid from an unbiased quarter — from counsellors.

Those who had abortions in NHS hospitals did not seem to have been offered any counselling at all. Those who went to non-profit making charity-run clinics did receive counselling but often, they felt, not enough.

Time is inevitably limited in these situations. Despite claims to the contrary from the anti-abortion lobby, no woman is likely to want a late abortion. Circumstances may have prevented her from acknowledging her pregnancy earlier (in the case of young girls, fear is a particularly strong factor). Or it may be inner conflict, or an unexpected change of circumstances which cause a decision to be made later rather than sooner. But, for most women suffering this dilemma, the relentless ticking of the clock is at the forefront of their minds.

Counselling is probably not the right word to use to describe the conversations that may occur between a woman and her doctor when the subject of abortion is first raised. Doctors decide whether or not a woman is eligible for abortion, but they are not necessarily trained to talk about feelings, although some doctors do have the natural empathy that enables them to do so. Many may speak from a personal position on abortion which makes it difficult for them to be objective. Certainly a number of women said that the reaction of the clinic or doctor coloured their own view of their pregnancy and, sometimes, limited their vision.

Counselling is therefore likely to be restricted to those attending pregnancy advisory clinics and other agencies, where the service is routine. But even there each woman may only be offered 15 minutes in which to express her state of mind. Also the content of the counselling session may vary not only from clinic to clinic but from counsellor to counsellor. The emphasis may be 'does this woman know what she is doing?' rather than 'what does this woman feel about what she is planning to do?' The need for more or better counselling right at the start, as an aid to decision-making, was expressed by most of the women I spoke to.

Catherine, who at 35 wanted her baby and was devastated by her boyfriend's inability to 'come clean' about his own wants and feelings, very much regrets that she didn't have any professional counselling at all. Nick had at no point showed excitement or pride or enthusiasm about the baby. Their relationship, though important to each of them, was unsettled; they lived in different towns and spent only weekends together; they had made no real commitment to each other — although, with the pregnancy, that was what Catherine was hoping for.

'At the outset, I had felt positive and excited about the baby but, simultaneously, frightened of Nick's reaction,' she said. 'I thought of the baby as something that had to involve both of us. I didn't want a baby on my own.

'I didn't want to be a single parent. I knew I *could* do it. I had a good job and I could let a room in my flat and even have a lodger for babysitting. It was all feasible. But I didn't want to do it. On the negative side, having little family, I could expect little practical or emotional support.

'For that reason, I felt it would be unfair to the child. And also, I felt cowardly. I might be inadequate and clingy and who was I to think I was able to bring up a child on my own? There was a lot of fear there.'

All these were first thoughts, however, before Catherine had told Nick she was pregnant. She was hoping for a positive response from him, and only when it became clear that he could not find the courage to commit himself did she have to give serious thought to the less desirable possibilities open to her. She went to see her doctor.

'The doctor had very strong views about one-parent families. He said they were terrible and that I should have an abortion. He said Nick would go off and leave me if we did go ahead.

'He was a very opinionated man and he even used to rant about how unreliable the diaphragm is. He put me down as yet another statistic for cap failure. I had pretended to him that I had used the diaphragm and the pregnancy was an accident. I was too frightened to say I sort of did it on purpose. I just knew what his reaction would be.

'I do wish now he hadn't been so negative. It coloured my attitude at the start. He didn't say, "ooh, you're not so old", etc. If he had, it might have been the support I needed at the time.'

She wishes, too, that she had, at that time, been in more regular contact with a friend who happens to be a single parent. But their lives had moved apart and their friendship didn't get re-established till much later. 'This friend feels now that she could have given me confidence. Whenever I'm with her she makes me feel good. She was the very person who could have shown me the other side of it!'

She was grateful, however, for the understanding of other friends. One even pointed out to her that she had always wanted a child and she was not the sort who normally had 'accidents'. If she didn't go ahead now, she would probably never let the possibility arise again.

'And she was right, in a way,' said Catherine. 'I've since had the coil fitted, so my body can't have its way even if it wanted to. I do wish I had had pregnancy counselling. I never had any professional counselling and I feel someone like that could have put the possibilities more objectively.

'I think that, if I had had counselling, I would have felt more certain about my decision, whatever it was. I would have felt that I had left no stone unturned. But, again, that is my character. I don't even buy a television without reading the *Which* Report.

'And yet I missed that step. I knew counselling existed but I was too emotional by then to do anything about finding any. There was one stage when I thought we had decided we were going to have the baby and it was a tremendous shock, the next weekend, when Nick backed out again. It was a bolt out of the blue. I just made my decision to have an abortion there and then and started to make the arrangements.

'A friend had a friend who was a counsellor. I spoke to her on the phone briefly once. She talked differently to me than friends did and I remember thinking, I really should have talked to someone like this. But it seemed all too late. The abortion by then had all been set up. It seemed like, "What's the point?"'

The point, as two counsellors explain in Chapter 7, is

that, even when the decision is made, a woman can benefit from being allowed to have her feelings — her grief, her anger, her regret. All too often, because abortion is seen as a choice, pain and sad feelings are considered inappropriate.

Joanne, whose Catholic boyfriend Ben refused to discuss the possibility of keeping the baby and who, in fact, could not bring himself to talk about the dilemma at all, did receive counselling. But when she talked to the woman doctor who had confirmed the pregnancy, then to the counsellor, she found herself over-emphasising the difficulties of her situation and later wished she had been challenged.

'I had lost my excitement, after Ben's reaction, and when we had returned from our holiday in the country, where he refused to mention the pregnancy again, I was feeling negative.

'I told the doctor that I was only 22, did shift-work, had no home and everything was chaotic. I think I was saying all that because I was basically going to ask for an abortion. So I was putting forward the negatives.'

In herself, however, she was still far from decided. Like Catherine, she had a friend who was a single parent but, unlike Catherine, she was able to see her. She had been longing, while still on the holiday, to get back and talk to this friend, as already she was trying to contemplate being a single parent. But, feeling ground down by Ben's negativity by the time she got back, she was so upset and distressed when she met her friend that she was unable to think about positives.

She was also facing her own conflicting feelings about having an abortion. 'A friend of mine had had an abortion when we were both students together. That seemed all right to me. I had campaigned for the right to have abortions. But, although I felt we should have the right, I realised I never wanted to have to use that right myself. I didn't want to become a person who had had an abortion.

'My doctor told me I wouldn't qualify for one on the NHS and gave me the address of an advisory service. I made an appointment and then it seemed as if I had taken the decision just by setting matters in motion. Certainly no one around me was making plans to have the baby. I thought at that stage that I had better have the abortion quickly or else I'd feel worse.

'The night before I went to the clinic, I stayed with my single mother friend and I realised then for sure that I *didn't* want a child on my own. I wanted to work, to get a place of my own to live. It would all stop if I had the baby. My friend certainly hadn't found it easy on her own.'

At the clinic, she saw a counsellor and realised that she was still in conflict about the abortion, despite her strong feelings the night before.

'It was all too easy,' she said. 'I felt I wanted someone to make it difficult for me. The counsellor accepted all my reasons about shift-work, etc. I thought she would get me to question my motives, to look at the positives. I was 22, I had a career, I had a boyfriend. A baby was *possible*. But she seemed bothered by my housing problems.

'At the end, I was asked if I could come in the next day for the abortion. I said: "I can't. I just can't!" It was sort of stupid because I wanted it over quickly. And yet I couldn't handle it that quick.'

In effect, although Joanne received counselling, she did not have a chance to explore her negative and sad feelings about abortion or her fears about whether it was the right decision. As many women feel obliged to do, she stressed the negatives of her situation in order not to reduce her chances of being granted an abortion. It was Joanne, however, who realised later, in a post-abortion therapy group, that, for her, a baby had symbolised a home and that her unconscious need had been for a home, not a baby. Pregnancy forced that conflict to the surface but she was still not conscious of it at the pre-abortion counselling stage, when it might have helped her to understand her predicament.

Her difficulties in exploring her feelings fully were inevitably compounded by Ben's inability to acknowledge or share what was happening. He was ashamed of himself for their being in their current dilemma at all and, in blocking it out himself, sometimes obliged her to block it out as well.

'The day before the abortion, we spent the evening with a couple we knew. The woman had herself had an abortion and I wanted to tell her about it. But I couldn't because I knew Ben would be so embarrassed. That night, however, when we were on our own, I did get Ben to mourn the baby. I made him put his hand on my stomach and I said: "This baby is here now. It won't be tomorrow. I want you to say goodbye to it."

'It was the only time he connected with it really. It was very important to me that he did because otherwise it was all just happening to me and he was completely apart from it. What would have helped was if someone had counselled us *both*.'

Claire, who was expected to support her 22-year-old husband Anthony through his studies for a higher degree, had a very different experience of counselling. Anthony had left the decision to Claire, then also 22, but she was in no doubt that he did not want the child, which would put an end to his study plans.

Claire said: 'I feel the counsellor reached the fine line between advising and persuading — persuading me to have the child. She pointed out that I could get a child-minder, carry on college to get my degree before getting a job, etc. I couldn't face it. I wasn't ready to have a child. I felt I had one on my hands already because of Anthony's need for my support. I felt sure that I would be dumped at some time if I did have the baby.

'I didn't say that to the counsellor though. I was adamant. I said we had no secure place to live, no income, nothing to give the child. So she referred me to a gynaecologist at an NHS hospital.

'I think I did have regrets and sadness. I was coming round to the possibility that I might perhaps want children. I couldn't express these feelings adequately to Anthony because it would have put his life in compromise. I subjugated my life to his in so many ways.'

She did feel that the counselling she received wasn't enough to be helpful. 'Effectively, the woman pushed me, I said no and she said okay. But there wasn't the time to go into feelings anyway. You have to make the decision so quickly, because of the weeks adding up, and the counselling session itself is only about 20 minutes.

'Perhaps it could only be helpful if the session were an hour or more and if counsellors were prepared to get more involved — to say "this *matters* what you decide now" rather than just putting the options and giving information, so that people make up their own minds.

'There is a level at which the counsellors remain uninvolved. I don't think they should force someone to do something they don't want to do; but to explore more avenues and be able to invite or handle the consequences of someone's emotions — the tears, the anger.'

At that time in her life, she feels, she was not in touch with her feelings at all and a brief counselling session could inevitably offer little. 'But if I had been asked to go back for follow-up counselling, I might have got more sense of myself. The feelings about the abortion might not have got buried so deep.' It was only after lengthy therapy, started some years later, that she uncovered what feelings she did have about the abortion.

Her resolve to have an abortion was in fact strengthened, after her counselling session, by the unsympathetic treatment she received from the gynaecologist she was referred to for examination.

'He was horrid. He treated me like a piece of meat and then really told me off. He said he would only consider abortion at all because I had been depressed. I had to be grateful he would even condescend to see me. I felt so ashamed but, also, angry. That behaviour made me the more determined to go ahead.'

Gillian, who, at 19, had not acknowledged her first pregnancy to herself till three months, also felt badly treated by medical staff. 'At the clinic where I went for the test, some staff were nice and some judgmental. It really makes a difference about how you feel about yourself. The first time, for the test, they were nice. When I went back, after thinking for a week, I saw a really horrible woman doctor. I felt I had to grovel and express guilt to get a letter for an abortion, so the decision was made. I felt I couldn't have expressed reservations.

'There was no counselling. She just said: "How come you didn't know till now? Why have you left it so late? Well, I suppose I'll *try* for a bed." She gave me a letter to take to an NHS hospital. I was 13 weeks by then. I had asked about private clinics but the doctor didn't know anything about them.

'I decided, at that point, that I would try to go privately because it would be quicker. But it was really hard finding out where to go.

'Abortion was a hard decision to accept and it wasn't because I unconsciously wanted a child. I was involved in student politics and animal rights and I just kept thinking, "what's the point in it all if here I am killing a baby?" I felt a hypocrite.

'I remember one night putting Rob's hand on my tummy and he pulled it away. I felt lonely, rejected and trapped, while he could take his hand away. He said he didn't want to get too involved with it, whereas I had no choice. It was in me.'

It was only after the abortion that she eventually sought counselling and was first able to identify what was going on for her at the time. It became very clear to her that the pregnancy, while causing its own conflict, was itself a manifestation of an existing but hidden conflict.

'The conflict in me was not over having the baby. It was that I had been hiding for so long and this had brought me face to face with myself. I had, till then, refused to take responsibility for things or make decisions.'

For Joyce, with a grown-up son and five months' pregnant after a sterilisation failure, the conflict was that she did not want a child and also did not approve of abortion. But the support she received from her husband and her friends was of more help to her than counselling, although the latter was sympathetic.

'I was in turmoil because, despite my feelings, I was convinced an abortion was what had to be right for me. So many things ran round in my head. Is it right? Is it cruel? I talked to Richard and to friends and I never backtracked on the decision to have an abortion, but I was anxious about the pain to the baby. The doctor said it would be born dead but I couldn't bear to think that it would be fully formed. Once I knew the brain wasn't formed properly, I felt a bit better.'

She and second husband Richard, who had no children, had agreed on abortion. They were referred to a charity-run clinic, although the health authority would be paying for the abortion as a sterilisation had gone wrong. In the health authority's own hospitals, the agreed time limit for abortions was only 16 weeks.

'Richard came with me to the clinic but the counsellor insisted he stayed outside, at least to start with. She said that some women felt under pressure from their partners to have an abortion and so it was important for them to have the chance to express their own views alone. I was surprised about that.

'She asked if I had children. She was sweet but I think she must have realised quite quickly that I was of sound mind and my mind was made up. I felt okay at the clinic, not hassled, got at or stared at. Everyone was very nice. There was another girl waiting and we just got chatting.

'But for me personally the counselling wasn't very important. I think my questions and concerns about whether I was doing the right thing were answered by talking to my own friends.'

She does feel very strongly, however, that a counsellor should be available in the actual clinic where the abortion is done, at the time of the operation (see Chapter 4).

Anna, whose baby had been diagnosed prenatally, at 20 weeks, as suffering from thalassaemia, wishes very strongly that counselling had been available to her. It is common practice for parents to be phoned with the results of prenatal diagnosis immediately that they are available. There is no face to face discussion about what to do.

'The doctors are very friendly and sympathetic,' said Anna. 'But they give you no guidance as to what to do. I must admit I would have liked someone to say, "it's a good idea to terminate in your position". Instead they just say, "there's a bed here if you want it".

'Even if you have decided beforehand that, if the baby is affected, you will terminate, when it comes to the crunch it isn't that easy.

'At the time it is all happening, you really don't know how to help yourself. You need to be *offered* help. If it had been offered to me or a support group drawn to my attention, I think it would have helped me.'

In 1988, a specialised support group was, in fact, established in England, especially to help women who find that their baby will be abnormal and who choose termination. A similar group exists in Scotland. (See Chapter 8 for addresses.)

Maria was the one woman who had high praise for the therapeutic help she received when deciding on abortion. It was not, however, counselling of the kind so far discussed; she had already been having individual therapy sessions for about six months before the pregnancy occurred.

Maria and Stuart had only known each other seven months but had decided to have their baby, despite much anxiety. Stuart had just become self-employed and neither one had accommodation big enough for them both to live in with a baby. When the stresses they both felt started to drive them apart, they decided after all on abortion. Again, Maria's memory is detailed as she kept a diary of the time.

'The decision had come as an enormous relief,' she said, 'as it had seemed as if our relationship was going to end. Stuart felt unable to go through with having the baby after all but at first also felt he couldn't stay with me after an abortion, as he is so strongly against it. It felt to me as if there was no way anything could now work out right, so to agree on abortion *and* staying together was a tremendous release from conflict.

'The stress of the last week or two had been almost unbearable, with our rowing and our own personal fears and reservations about going ahead. On the morning we made our decision, we felt so lightened and so close.

'The next day, however, he rang me and sounded low. But he said he was just feeling tired and felt like staying in. It was a Saturday night. Alarm bells started ringing. He heard the anxiety in my voice and agreed to meet me.

'We went for a drink and he was very withdrawn. He finally admitted that that afternoon he had cried, for the first time in years, for what might have been and he didn't think we could survive it after all. My heart went cold. He must have seen my pain too because suddenly he was able to reach out for me again. We talked and he decided he *could* cope with our decision. Again I was relieved and I didn't dare look any further than that.

'The Sunday evening, which we were spending together, he had to pop out and at that moment a friend rang. She is a psychotherapist and the one who had first suggested I try some therapy, with a colleague of hers. She was shocked at my news. "Are you sure it isn't fear and panic? Couldn't you have a child for yourself? It is such a deep thing, abortion. Are you sure it can't be resolved?" She made me book a special session with Sally, my therapist. I think I had been avoiding doing that, trying to bury my head in the sand about any conflicting feelings.

'By the time Stuart returned, all my fear had come back. All my feelings about the baby must have been suppressed till then and now they were all churning around inside. But this time it was he who felt firmly our decision was right. The next day, for me, was agonising. What could have been, what could still be, what I was about to do, all pounded in my mind. Every mother with a child in the street caused me grief. I just felt panic, turmoil, despair.

'I started to feel a coward too. But Stuart was still strong. It was as if he had resolved his own conflicts on the Saturday night. He assured me he would be there for me afterwards, after the abortion. One of my fears was that he might find himself unable to do that.

'I made the arrangements for two days later, with Judy, the friend who was the matron of an abortion clinic. I felt calm by then although not trusting my feelings weren't blocked. The next day I had my special appointment to see Sally, on a day she didn't normally work. It felt comforting that I was important enough for her to want to do that.

'It was the most upsetting session. She was trying to make me look at why I couldn't have the child on my own (she herself had been left as a single parent very soon after her own baby was born). All I could reach, however, was panic — even though I knew, at some level, that of course I could manage, if Sally was any example, and perhaps I might grow, as she certainly had done, whereas down this route (abortion) lay only emptiness. Sally cried with me and begged me to put the decision off for a week, to be sure of what I was doing. I was only eight weeks' pregnant.

'My psychotherapist friend also rang that evening with the same request. She just felt abortion would be so bad for me.

'I remember lying in the bath feeling battered by the emotions of caring others. I suddenly couldn't get to any feelings of my own any more. Then, as I was sitting waiting for Stuart in the evening, I had a real as opposed to a romantic flash of what it would be like to go it alone — and knew deeply I didn't want to do it.

'Stuart and I went to a wine bar. We were both subdued. We talked of how terrible it felt that any of this had happened and how we would only win through, as a couple, if we wanted to enough. Stuart rarely cries but that night, in bed, he burst into racking sobs and turned away from me to cry. I found myself first going numb and then letting my own sorrow go. He turned to me, held me and we both grieved together.

'To say I am grateful for such pain sounds strange. But I am so grateful that Sally and my psychotherapist friend did not let me suppress my feelings. That, by pulling the other way — not to make me have a baby but to make me explore all my feelings about having a baby and question my assumptions — I went through every possible emotion I could have experienced. When I went and had an abortion the following day, I still felt excruciatingly sad and regretful. But I was fully responsible for and conscious about my decision.'

Grace, whose doctor and mother had arranged her (illegal) abortion was not conscious of making any decision, and she regrets that. 'I was in a daze and simply followed down the path they were leading me. I was only 19. I don't know if I would have had an abortion, given options. I would have examined very carefully whether it was possible for me to have that child. I might still have had an abortion but at least I would have thought carefully about it. But there was no opportunity to talk or think. Everything was just put in motion.'

What seems to come out of all this is that most women want the chance to make a conscious, responsible decision; to know that all conflicting feelings have been unearthed and explored, if necessary away from the influence of partners or family.

Neither the time nor the resources are available for protracted abortion counselling before the event. But women can at least be pointed in the right emotional direction, even within the limited time available. Obviously none of the women quoted here decided against abortion. But being given 'permission' to rage, to weep, to regret, to mourn, may often be sufficient to start the healing process that must follow.

4.
ENDINGS
The experience of abortion

The day of the abortion is usually dreaded. Even if a woman
has made up her mind that what she is doing is right or
necessary, it is a day she would rather not have to live
through. Those who are less sure of themselves find their
conflicting feelings relentlessly following them to the clinic
or hospital ward. A woman's emotions may be so deep that
they colour her perception of the actual procedure and
place. Curtains and furnishings in a clinic may be reported
as being dirty, for instance, when in fact they are not.

Certainly the experience itself is vested with a range of
varying emotions. Inevitably there is anxiety. Some
women may feel cut off and alone, others uncomfortably
part of a herd. The attitudes of the staff have strong
effects on the way a woman sees herself, both before and
after the operation.

Comfort is often desperately needed and yet not
forthcoming (or not seen as forthcoming) and perhaps not
even sought. A woman who has an abortion is not ill. She
has 'chosen' to undergo an operation which is the very
opposite of life-giving. An unconscious part of her may
even feel she doesn't deserve much sympathy or support.

Afterwards, immediate reactions may be very different
from those expected — relief instead of misery, deadness
instead of relief.

Only a few women I spoke to had any unexpectedly
positive memories of any part of the experience. It is no
surprise, perhaps, that one of them was Andrea, the 32-

year-old who knew she wanted children more than anything in the world and yet experienced her first accidental pregnancy as an 'evil' inside her. She had been determined to have an abortion and had arranged one extremely quickly. She went into an NHS hospital as a private patient.

She said: 'I had told the doctor when I first saw him that I would rather go home than stay overnight. He said I would probably want to stay, so I didn't argue. On the day, I was nervous because I had never had any operation or been in hospital before. But I also felt relieved and happy that the day had come. I can't remember any moments of doubt. If I did have any, they must have been fleeting.'

Her description of the events as she perceives them is completely positive, reflecting perhaps her own state of mind. She had felt no guilt or shame at her pregnancy, just a pervading sense of being dirtied and needing to be cleansed. She was not critical of herself and felt no criticism levelled at her.

'I remember,' she says, 'that a nurse came and gave me a needle in my arm and then I slowly passed out and then slowly came round and everyone was looking after me. I remember feeling high at some point and that I didn't mind all this at all. The nurses and the food and everything were wonderful. In fact, it was all very pleasurable. I had a room of my own, a TV, no pain.

'The surgeon told me, afterwards, that the foetus was only five weeks old and the operation was easier than a scrape. He told me I would have no problems getting pregnant again. I walked out in the morning, feeling as if it was spring and I had been reborn. I got on with my life and never gave it a second thought.

'I felt I had done it right. I was glad I had been lucky enough to afford to go privately, to get it all done quickly.'

Maria, too, felt positive about her treatment at the clinic she went to (her circumstances were unusual) but by no means positive emotionally. She and Stuart, who had first decided they would have their child, had, a month later, decided they could not go through with it.

'On the morning of the operation, I was to be collected by Judy, my friend who was the matron at the clinic, and was to travel there with her. I recall getting up at 7 am to get ready while Stuart stayed in bed. I sat down beside him and he held me and said: "Do you want to go?" I said no, but I couldn't have not gone either.

'I remember travelling in the car and Judy trying to be sort of cheerful but I wasn't really listening. When we got there, I went with Judy and sat in her office while she dealt with immediate things she had to sort out. It was strange receiving such priority treatment. People came in and were friendly, as if I were a visitor. But it was hard to respond. The night matron came in to hand over. I had met her before, at a party the clinic had held the previous summer. I was glad she didn't remember. When she realised I was a friend, she was quite apologetic that she wouldn't be on that night to cheer me up. I think, in fact, I felt relieved by that. I was receding into myslef by that stage.

'Eventually I ended up in the queue with all the other girls, waiting to pay our money and then be examined. Most were not English. There was a pained atmosphere in that first room. It was too small for everyone to have a seat. No one but the administrator spoke.

'When I went for my examination, the doctor could not get blood from my veins. This has happened to me a lot before and it is never very pleasant. When you think it is all over, they haven't even started and have to jab at you several times. On this occasion, I found my nerves couldn't stand it. I wanted to scream at him to stop and started to cry, I think. Eventually he had to abandon it until the anaesthetist saw me later.

'All the rooms were either single or doubles, no wards. I had a single and I was very grateful. I don't remember much more about the before, except that I went down barefoot in a lift with a nurse. Then I was on a trolley in recovery, Judy was smiling at me and I was in floods of tears. She said that was just reaction and I would be all right very soon.

'I remember nothing more till I was back in bed in my room with a pad between my legs. Judy came in with a beautiful bunch of freesias she had bought me and gave me a kiss. I really felt very cared for by her. She kept coming in and out to me through the day. Later, in the evening, I wrote down all that had happened from discovering my pregnancy to this point, and my feelings.

'I felt very subdued. A slight pain and a sort of flatness in my stomach and in my heart. The room itself felt womblike and time was suspended inside it. A doctor came and told me the foetus was only eight weeks. I remember thinking I hadn't said goodbye, everything had seemed to happen so fast.

'I thought, what comes next? How strange to have spent a month feeling the pregnantness, the pride and the fear, the awareness of childbirth and children and now, nothing.

'I knew I wasn't feeling and wished I could feel. I imagined Stuart feeling wrenched and anxious and grieving while I just sat hot and numb, lost in space, breathing unsteadily with panic below the surface.

'I wrote: "It is very deep, so deep I have lost touch with it again. Who am I anymore? Not a potential mother and nurturer. Just a selfish individual. I suppose there is a relief in me. But I feel at the mercy of a massive misery that must at some time crush me. I don't even mind staying here in this cocoon of a room, alone, not facing the world and the responsibilities that are about families and growth. I have chosen against life."

'It was all pretty dramatic and soul-searching. I had plenty of time for that, in the room that night, long after Judy had gone home. My psychotherapist friend came up specially to see me and again I felt very cared for. She, who had feared my decision was wrong, was there to express love and support. It was she who suggested I write everything down.

'That evening, too, Stuart rang. He was upset and concerned and subdued but his call was an enormous relief. My biggest fear had been that he might not be there for me the next night. It hadn't occurred to either of us that he could visit. I don't think it could have been what either of us wanted.

'In the morning, having taken a taxi home and walked into my lovely, familiar front room, I felt only relief. A bursting, joyful relief that the terrible weeks of agony and indecision were over.'

Whereas Maria felt enormously lucky to have received such personal and caring treatment (it was not only her friend but other nurses and care staff who seemed kindly), Joanne felt only indifference from the staff and aloneness, despite the fact that there were plenty of other women patients around her.

'Ben came with me to the centre. I was scared. I had never had an operation before and I didn't want this particular operation to happen. But I had set it all up and saw it as all too late now,' she said.

'I shared a room with a younger girl. She was Irish, only about 18 and she kept talking about her large family and all their children. She said: "I'm too young now but when I'm 23, I'd like a family." I felt terrible. I was nearly 23 and I felt so selfish. Materially, I had more going for me than she would probably have at 23, and yet I was having an abortion.'

The indifference she saw in the staff was epitomised by the following incident: 'Before they give you your injection, they ask your name, I couldn't say it. I didn't want to be associated with what was happening. I cried. A nurse said: "Don't you want the operation?" I said, "Why, is there someone I could speak to?" "No," she said. "But we can't do the operation if your nose is blocked." So I said: 'I'd better blow it then," and that was the last I remember.

'When I came round, I felt deadened. Not relieved. Then it was like being in a girls' school. Everyone was talking about their physical feelings and aches — and yet we had all avoided talking about our emotional feelings the night before, when our babies were alive. Everyone of us.

'Then the men came, looking sheepish. Ben brought me

chrysanthemums. He was uncomfortable but relieved. Like, we could forget all about this now.' It was Ben, who, as a Catholic, had had difficulty in acknowledging the pregnancy or the impending abortion any more than he was forced to.

Joanne's sensation that she and all the other women were suppressing their real feelings and were, therefore, incapable of offering or receiving comfort persisted the next day.

'That morning, at breakfast, no one mentioned why we were there. There were 30 of us together, saying things like "pass the toast", nothing else. It was very strange. I don't know if I really wanted to talk or not, because I don't know what I wanted to say. Then everyone shot away very quickly. There were no goodbyes.

'Ben picked me up and we stayed at his flat and then came and spent the night at my parents' house. Ben was okay, fairly caring. I wasn't crying or upset because I knew he couldn't have handled that. Also, I didn't want to think about it much myself because, if I did, I wanted to cry.'

Gillian, three months' pregnant, had a very similar awareness of the atmosphere in the clinic that she went to. 'I was put in a six-bedded ward and I read a whole book without taking a word of it in. A lot of the others were talking but they never mentioned abortion. It felt such a bizarre situation. I didn't want to talk to anyone at all.

'After that, I only recall lying in stirrups and really wishing it could have been Rob going through this, not me. It's irrational but I felt it. When I came round, I had a pain in my tummy. I felt nothing really except "that's it". It had all been so clinical. I had no relief at that stage.

'But I did feel as if something had been taken away and I was on my own again. It was a weird feeling. Rob was at work and couldn't come to pick me up the next day, so my male friend (who, although anti-abortion, had turned out to be very supportive) picked me up and took me to his house. I still felt nothing.'

For Diana, three times a mother and then 41, it was again the atmosphere generated by the women at the clinic that stands out in her memory. The procedure she only recalls as 'pretty standard' but she was struck by the difference in atmosphere the first and second time she had an abortion, and the effect that had on her. Her experience, the first time, was very different from that recalled by Gillian and Joanne.

'The first time was when my first marriage was on the rocks and I was pregnant by a lover whom I had just broken up with. I was very emotional about him but I was going to have another try at my marriage.

'I remember being terribly apprehensive when I reached the clinic and there were a lot of us in the ward together. Afterwards, the feeling of relief was almost tangible. We formed instant friendships and even exchanged addresses.

'The second time that didn't happen. Whereas the first time we had all stayed the night, the second time I went to a hospital for a day abortion, under local anaesthetic. I felt as if I was just passing through. The women there for abortion were in separate cubicles and then we were leaving virtually straight away. Reacting with relief and laughter just didn't come into it. I was less depressed after the first abortion than after the second.'

Claire also had two contrasting experiences, but both of them left her feeling bad and guilty about herself. The first time she was only 19.

'I had been sent to a private clinic and had a private room. Most of the women were foreign. I remember having to turn up early in the morning and feeling apprehensive.

'The staff treated me briskly. I felt as if I was on a conveyor belt, especially when I came round in the recovery room and saw other women there on trolleys beside me. There was a jolly black nurse from an agency. But the fact that she was from an agency made me feel that she, and other nurses, were there just for the money. It wasn't a vocation, working there.

'In my private room, I saw no one and spoke to no one. I felt very lonely. Anthony came in the evening and I felt distant, as if he were some kind of intruder in a very female world.'

The second abortion, at 22 when she and Anthony were married and she was unsure about wanting a child, was a far more vividly awful experience.

'I don't recall my feelings,' she said, 'but I remember the ward, this time in a hospital. I had a bed right at the far end, next to an old lady with cancer of the cervix. She was senile and incontinent. I helped with her a lot.

'Other women there were having hysterectomies or sterilisations. One young woman had fibroids, another was there because she was bleeding during pregnancy. I found it difficult to say what I was in for. But the nurses were kindly.

'I recall being wheeled in to see a young doctor. He examined me and I said I thought I was eight to 10 weeks. He said "Oh no, far more than that". He was very unpleasant. He said — and it has stayed with me for the last 10 years — "You do realise that if you have this abortion you may never be able to carry another child?"

'I remember panicking. Part of me wanted to stop it there and then. He was horrid, brusque. From that point on I was worried.

'I had to stay in for a few days. I can't remember why, and I was shaved. All the women on the ward called it the Kojak. Yet those who had women doctors didn't have to be shaved. It was humiliating and embarrassing.

'Anthony came each day, looking steadily more delapidated and haggard. It was obvious that, without me, he wasn't looking after himself. The whole thing was a bit nightmarish. I recall nurses washing me and sanitary towels and the effects of the anaesthetic. Then, a few days later, I felt a lot better. I'm sure I had been in there about five days by then. I was waiting for Anthony to take me home and I fainted.

'My temperature shot up and I bled heavily. I wasn't even allowed to go to the loo on my own because I was delirious. I had got an infection and I had to have a D & C back in the theatre.

'I felt totally bewildered. I can't remember making any sense of things. I must have been there 12 days altogether and I felt almost frightened to leave hospital. At least things were ordered in there. I didn't, for once, have to take responsibility.

'But I now firmly believed, especially after the fever, that I couldn't ever have children. I still had my ambivalent feelings about whether I wanted children, but I felt terribly sad no longer to have the option. In fact, I still don't know whether it's true.'

For Catherine, the decision to arrange an abortion had been made immediately that Nick started vacillating yet again about having their baby. She lost all trust in him and acted almost mechanically. 'I felt "to hell with you, Nick, I've just got to do something on my own". He opted out of the whole business and that tells its own story. I was just being practical by then.

'I felt desperately unhappy the day I went to the private clinic. Really, really terrible. It was all under sufferance. Right up till the last minute, I didn't want to do it and it was only iron will power that got me through. I was revolted.

'It didn't occur to me to say goodbye to the baby. I was so upset. My last few thoughts were, "get me in there quickly or any minute I'll go home". If they had kept me waiting another half an hour, I might well have got up and gone. But it's too late for regret now.

'When I came round from the anaesthetic, I couldn't believe it was done. I thought I hadn't been in. Then I felt a pad between my legs and thought, "God, they've done it!" It seemed like seconds.

'I felt enormous instant relief. At that point, there were no regrets. The main thing was there was no more agonising. It was done. I didn't feel tearful. I felt I could relax for the first time in seven weeks. I had been nine weeks' pregnant. I felt peaceful and I don't remember crying. I felt as if I didn't have to think anymore. There was nothing to think about.'

As for many women, her instant relief was the relief from indecision, from being wrenched unbearably in two directions. Her main memory of the procedure itself, however, was a lack of common humanity and comfort from the staff. 'Before it had happened, I broke down and cried in front of doctors and nurses. They didn't say anything or respond in any way. I think it was a case of write your cheque and get on with it.'

She felt a bitterness akin to that felt by Joanne when told that she couldn't have her operation if she blocked her nose by crying. And it was a bitterness very fiercely shared by Joyce, 39 and over five months' pregnant after a failed sterilisation. Her abortion is very recent and her memories detailed and hostile.

'I was so shocked and concerned by the lack of emotional support in the clinic, apart from that offered by other women patients,' she said. 'It's like, I have an old aunt who lives in a home for the elderly and I was appalled there one day to see a staff member washing and feeding an old woman without a single word to show caring or acknowledge she was there. I felt the same way about the clinic.'

Joyce had known very definitely that she did not want another child and had been understandably angry and upset that, after taking the care to have a sterilisation, she should find herself in her current position. She had always been anti-abortion.

'On the morning that I was to go to the clinic I felt terrible. I woke up in panic,' she said. 'I decided I couldn't breathe because my nose felt very blocked. I was very upset and terrified of going through with it.

'It was a Sunday and Christmas was the following Friday. Yet I couldn't see anything beyond that Sunday. I seemed to stop — my life seemed to stop there, that is.

'I was too upset to talk in the car. I remember Richard driving us through town at 7am and I was feeling, "This is my last day on earth". I just couldn't see anything at all beyond that day and I've never felt like that before in my life. It was weird and frightening, like a death feeling.

'At the clinic, the waiting room was packed. We registered and sat down, and then I was taken upstairs and shown the ward. I have been specially moved to a corner because I had arranged before that Richard would be allowed up there with me for a while.

'I undressed and sat there. In fact we all just sat there like monkeys until suddenly one girl was told by a nurse to go to the loo and then 15 minutes later she came back on a trolley!

'It knocked us all for six because no one told us we were starting to go down to theatre. The nurses had brought round a leaflet on contraception but gave us no other information! After a little while, everyone in my ward had gone down except me. I was sitting there alone and they still wouldn't let me see Richard. I was very emotional and badly needed support. But no.

'Eventually a nurse said to me, "Two more day patients and then you". I felt so isolated. In fact, I'd felt isolated, like as if I was in a glass case, ever since I discovered the pregnancy. The clinic just accentuated the "you are in this thing on your own, kid" kind of feeling.

'I was taken down by foot to outside the theatre and left sitting by a whole load of hypodermic syringes. They don't happen to bother me but just imagine! I was really howling my head off by now but no one said a word of comfort. The staff were inhuman. In fact, if I had known how to get out of that operating theatre, I'd have run, though I don't know why, as I didn't want the child.

'Half of me was saying all day, in that clinic, "This isn't right". It didn't change my decision yet I had a fundamental feeling of doing wrong. It felt as if I was two different people.

'There was no pre-med. A doctor put his head round a curtain and said, "How are you?" I burst into tears again and he just went away and then came back and said, "What's the matter with you?" I said, "Will someone *please* tell me what is going on?" The sister then told me that the surgeon would take a look at me.

'I was ushered into a room and up on to a table. The surgeon examined me and said he would be able to do the whole thing straight away, no drip. I had expected to be given prostaglandins to induce labour and then the next day have a D & C but the surgeon decided it wasn't necessary to induce.

'The anaesthetist seized my arm and I snatched it back in my fear and panic. He said, "Don't be such a baby. You are having an injection." I felt the finger was being pointed at me. I felt like screaming, "Look, I didn't choose to be here. I did everything I could to avoid this. I had a sterilisation!" And then it was all over.

'When I woke up, my first reaction was to wonder that I was still alive. My next was to think, "Where's everybody else? All the beds are empty. Am I in a dream?"

'I did feel relief that it was over. But I got more weepy and upset as the day went on. I looked at the clock. It was 1.30pm and I thought, "Oh God, Richard has been stuck downstairs since 8am". I got upset and panicky about that. And it was 4pm before a nurse even told me that he had been sent home at nine that morning!

'A second crop of girls had come in and I was terribly worried that they might just disappear and not return too. Then I started feeling angry. I felt it was unjust that they had to *pay* for this lousy service. (My operation was being paid for by my area health authority because the sterilisation they had been responsible for had been a failure.) I also felt that I shouldn't have had to go through all this in the first place.

'I still felt like screaming, "I never in a million years wanted to be here. Don't point the finger at me!" The nurses were so indifferent. It was like we were a rack of cattle. I was always referred to as "bed five" and that didn't help. They could at least have used first names to relax the atmosphere.

'Richard was finally let in at 5pm. He had gone home in floods of tears because he had told me he would be here and then he couldn't be. I felt so relieved to see him. I felt as if I had my right arm back. We didn't know why he hadn't been allowed to stay in the day, when the sister, on the phone beforehand, had said yes.

'He had to leave at 8pm but I felt a little easier after seeing him. The girl in the next bed to me started shaking and a nurse said to her, "I don't know why you are shaking. It's very expensive to call a doctor, you know. Oh, here's your husband. He'll cheer you up." So my attention got taken up with trying to care for and comfort the girl. I think it was only my *Punch* sense of humour that got me through it all.

'I also felt less anxious when I knew the second lot of girls were staying the night, like me, so I would have company. We all felt a bit worried about whether our operations had been done properly or whether we might still be pregnant. I started panicking about whether my baby had been born screaming and was thrown in an incinerator. I had to push all that terror away. I couldn't handle it then, although it has come back to me since.

'A doctor came round before discharge next day. It was a two-minute poke-poke and that was it. I was given no painkillers to take away and I was in excruciating agony a week later.

'But it was the lack of emotional support in the clinic that most disturbed me. There should be a counsellor there, on site. Or the staff should be a bit more humane. What would it have cost the staff nurse to tell me that Richard couldn't come up to the ward after all and he had gone home and would be back at 5pm? It would have saved me so much anxiety and panic.'

She summed up a lot of people's feelings when she said: 'I was very screwed up in there, with all my emotions — fear, disbelief, anxiety. It would have helped so much if someone had just thought to put an arm round me.'

Sarah's overriding memory of the day of her first abortion was also the attitude of a staff member, albeit one who perhaps meant to be kind and helpful. She was in an NHS hospital.

'I felt I was treated well but distantly. For myself I was feeling a bit ashamed. I was in pain when I came round and I wrote a poem. It was about the lurid physical parts, the clots of blood, that it had all come down to, and it was also a sad goodbye to the baby.

'I had actually been miscarrying for about a week before

the abortion. The clots had got bigger and bigger and I got really scared. I was relieved to be in hospital after that. A woman doctor came round afterwards and said, "There was nothing much left in there, dear. Only a few old bits."

'She was very matter of fact. I felt very discarded, like this baby didn't mean anything. I was shocked by her apparent ruthlessness — but also by my own.'

Unlike some women, who would have welcomed a miscarriage particularly as a way of relieving guilt or mixed feelings about an abortion, Sarah very firmly thinks of what happened to her as abortion.

'I think of it as abortion because I had decided to have one. And, because of that, it doesn't make any difference that it wasn't quite like that in the end,' she said.

That feeling was shared by Anna who had had two abortions after discovering she was carrying a thalassaemic child. 'The third time, the doctors actually caused a miscarriage by the prenatal testing, at around 16 weeks. I never knew the result. The baby was in an awkward position and eventually must have got damaged. They couldn't get any samples.

'By morning I had gone into labour and lost the baby. I had been offered the other diagnostic test, chorion villus sampling, which can be done at eight weeks. But it doesn't always give a conclusive result, so it seemed pointless having it. But if I had, maybe they *could* definitely have said the baby didn't have thalassaemia. I'll never know. So it was the late test, which I was responsible for choosing, that definitely caused miscarriage and so I view what happened as a third termination for that reason.'

The first abortion was the worst for her. In NHS hospitals, the normal procedure at the late stage is to induce labour.

'I felt petrified,' she said. 'I felt, this is some nightmare, some horror movie. My bed was booked for the day after we had received the diagnosis on the phone, so I didn't even have a chance to grieve.

'I didn't realise the full implications of going into labour, then. But, when it was all over, it really hit me. I had worked so hard in labour and afterwards I had nothing.

'Paul and I were too frightened to see the baby. Afterwards I felt that was a mistake. I saw the third baby and felt better for having seen it. But, the first and second time I was too frightened at what I would see at 20 weeks.

'The first time was definitely the worst. I was in an ordinary labour ward, so I could hear babies being born. Their first cries were heartwrenching. And there was I going away empty-handed.

'The labour took 24 hours and I stayed in an extra day. Paul was with me all the time and that helped me, although I can't put my finger on how, because I felt I had to look after him as well!

'I was relieved when it was all over. Then I felt really empty, lonely and very sad. I was very emotional. And I was in a daze. I wasn't sure if I had done the right thing. Even after three, I still feel guilty at taking a life. I'm not really in favour of abortion as such, so it feels a little hypocritical.

'The second time I didn't find it as difficult to say I'd have a termination as the first time. I did have slight doubts but felt I couldn't keep that one if I had got rid of the first. Somehow, it would have meant that the first was a terrible waste, a death for nothing, if, in the end, I was still going to be coping with a thalassaemic child.'

Joan, who had had one severely handicapped child die at the age of six and then was pregnant with another, had deliberately tried to detach her emotions from the pregnancy till she could have the test and knew whether the baby was normal or not. She and husband Steven hadn't hesitated over abortion.

'I had felt the baby kicking but I don't think that made it any harder to accept the termination, because I was so divorced from the baby. But it was pretty terrible going through labour for nothing at the end. My first child, who died, had taken 10 hours to be born. My second, who is now five, took half an hour. This one took 17 hours.

'The labour was very painful and I have a high pain threshold normally. The pain was much, much worse but I don't feel it was to do with the mental side. I feel it was because the baby wasn't ready for it. The baby was hanging on. Mentally I did feel prepared for it. But, then again, perhaps you can put up with more pain when you are expecting a live birth.

'There was no sensation of birth because the doctor put his hand in and pulled it out. He had asked before if we wanted to see it and we had said no. Afterwards, he said the cord was wrapped round its neck and its organs were macerated. He said it could never have survived. I felt so much better about that.

'I had no real sense of grief then, because I knew it had had no chance. But I felt absolutely alone afterwards. I was put in a room by myself. Steven went home because he was shattered, and no one came in to me at all.'

Where the abortion took place, in an NHS hospital or private clinic, seemed to have little bearing on the degree of distress the women suffered. Certainly there was a feeling that women were shifted through some private clinics at an alarming rate and treated with a lack of individuality. But in general, memories of the experience were coloured mainly by whether individual staff were caring or not, and by the state of mind of the woman herself.

The most frightening experience, shared, thankfully, by no one else I interviewed, was that undergone by Grace. She had an illegal abortion in South Carolina when she was 19, over 30 years ago. It was Grace who had felt dazed and completely under the control of others. Her doctor, who was a family friend, and her mother had decided on abortion, without reference to her, and she went along with it.

'The doctor, after much difficulty, had found us an address. It was a very risky business for him. We had to phone a certain number and use a special sort of wording. I can't remember exactly what but something to do with "services" rather than abortion. The person we had to ring was a sister someone. She told us to come at 10 in the morning. It was a black area right down in the slums, and we were told not to bring the car beyond a certain point as that would look suspicious. No one there had cars.

'She was a big brawny lady and her sitting room was cheap and sparse-looking. I was fearful and anxious about the unknown. I had no fear then about losing the baby.

'She took me into a bedroom, an ordinary bedroom with two twin beds. There was a statuette of the Virgin Mary on the wall and flowers on the table. A rubber sheet covered a white counterpane on one bed.

'I had to lie sideways and she put something up me and fiddled. It felt like wire with a loop at the top. She kept doing it for five or 10 minutes and the sensation was like a bad period pain. I was tense and uncomfortable.

'At that point, for the first time, the whole thing did take on nightmare proportions, in that seedy house with the big brawny woman. Eventually she said something like, "Well, that should do it. Go home and wait. It should come down in due course. Make sure you keep moving because that will bring it on."

'It made it all the worse, somehow, that my oh-so-conventional mother was having to participate in all this. But, for her, anything was better than a child out of wedlock. Better to tidy up the traces.

'We thanked the brawny lady profusely and paid her some enormous amount — I can't remember exactly what, but it was a hell of a lot. It put abortion out of court for most people at that time. Stunned and frozen as I was, I recall the woman saying, "Goodbye. If you ever need me again, you know where to find me." I thought, how could she be so casual. She made it so mundane and to me it was all so horrendous.

'We went back to the hotel room my mother had taken for the day. Our doctor had said that, as soon as there were any signs of bleeding, we should ring him and he would admit me to a proper hospital as a miscarriage case for a D & C. He didn't want to take any risks.

'At the hotel, my body started acting independently of my mind or, rather, it *knew* my mind. Because what I remember is that for 10 or 12 hours after we returned at 11.30am, no bleeding started. I realised I was pleased. But my mother was frantic to get me to the hospital and get it all over with.

'I remember lying curled up trying to hold on to that baby, once I realised nothing was happening. My mother was screaming, "Get up and walk!" and pouring gin into me. I hadn't known till that moment what *I* had wanted.

'At midnight the bleeding began and it was such a nightmare. I remember clearly, even now, the horror of it. My mother had bought me a cheap wedding ring and I went to hospital as young Mrs Thing. Once again I was caught up in a bustle of events. In the hotel, for that period, there had been a hiatus when I was myself.

'Presumably I wanted to lose the baby more than to keep it or I would have made a stand in the first place. But social and parental pressures then were very strong. I woke up in hospital feeling both tremendous relief and tremendous sadness.'

5.
FEELINGS
The aftermath, immediate and later

It has been said by some doctors, and by various other people, that abortion is pretty much akin to having a tooth pulled. But that is not a view shared by very many women who have experienced abortion for themselves. Unlike tooth-pulling, abortion is not necessarily over and done with once it is carried out. It carries emotional connotations, to do with life and death, with fertility and womanhood, sexuality and identity. For some, unconscious conflicts in these or other areas may have led to the pregnancy in the first place. For many more, they cause conscious conflict afterwards. Abortion can have a decisive impact on relationships with partners and with parents and on a woman's whole direction in life.

It is common for women to have a range of reactions to the experience of abortion, some that they experience immediately, some that may not manifest themselves till years later. It is also, however, not unusual for a woman to adjust, absorb and make sense quickly of what has happened to her and carry straight on with her life. Some are even able to draw something clear and positive from their experience, however difficult at the time, to carry into their futures.

Of the woman I spoke to, two did not feel able, or have the opportunity, to share their feelings afterwards with someone understanding, and both have a particularly strong sense that abortion has dramatically affected their lives.

Grace, 53, who had the illegal abortion aged 19 in South Carolina, and who only experienced her own desire to hold on to her child when it was too late, said: 'That abortion had *the* most serious effect on my life.'

Living in a society at a time when getting pregnant outside of marriage, to say nothing of illegal abortion, was highly taboo, she had felt unable to talk to anyone about the horrific experience of backstreet abortion and its emotional aftermath.

'I mourned that child for a long time,' she said. 'I had had no idea how I would feel at the time and I couldn't talk about it to anyone, least of all my mother, who, although she had been there through it at the time, now wanted it completely forgotten.

'I couldn't forget it. It took me four or five years to come to terms with it, by which time I had already made the catastrophic decision which was to affect my life.'

Grace had not been happy in her early family life. Her parents were white and privileged in the American South, and she had been brought up to expect to have whatever money and status could supply. She left home at 18 to try to live her own way instead.

'I hadn't liked the future they had mapped out for me and reacted against their fatuous, conventional, racist lifestyle. Away from home, I was starting to do my best to carve out a life that, for me, had more honesty. I was trying to work and, in my terms, be decent, whereas they still wanted me to be a carbon copy of them.'

At the time of her pregnancy, then, she was clearly in personal conflict, pulled one way by parental pressure and another by her own burgeoning beliefs and values in life. But, as she has said earlier, she had not yet experienced any really extreme shocks in her previously cushioned life. The abortion was that first shock and she had no one, bar herself, with whom to explore her feelings of confusion and guilt.

'After the abortion, I remember doubting a lot of my ideals about how I wanted to live my life. All the time I kept thinking to myself, "I've tried to do it my way and my way has led to a murder. At least, if I had done things *their* way, it wouldn't have come to that."

'So I gave up trusting myself and went home and married someone they approved of.' It was a disastrous marriage. She had a daughter (whom she feared might be damaged) but, unable to settle in a racist society she despised with a man she didn't love, she felt forced to leave a few years later. She took her daughter with her to New York but the father took back the child a year later, when Grace had had a virtual nervous breakdown. She was allowed to see little more of her daughter and eventually moved to England.

Now that her daughter has grown up and married they are in touch again. But her daughter's life has not been without severe emotional problems, for which Grace still feels strongly responsible.

'The abortion comes back to me even now sometimes, when I am reviewing my life,' she said. 'It stays with me as something I'm really sorry for happening. It is a personal grief, not triggered by outside things, like other people's babies. I adore other people's babies and look forward to grandchildren.

'It wasn't that the child was real to me, it was that I had terminated a potential life. It is more important than a feeling of "my child". It was that life was coming through my body and I interfered with that.

'It would have helped so much to have been able to talk about it. Only my mother and I knew it had happened and she refused to acknowledge it. It was such a stigma. If ever any of my younger friends now might be considering an abortion, I never talk them out of it but I say they should be prepared to have strong feelings about it afterwards.'

The only positive aspect of the experience that she can think of is one that she would rather have learned a different way: 'I learned that parts of oneself that one is not aware of have a very strong influence on behaviour.

'For instance, I don't know why I suggested pregnancy as well that day when I went to my doctor and he correctly diagnosed my appendicitis. It was as if I were seeking attention. Also, when I curled up after the backstreet abortionist had done her bit to induce abortion and didn't want to let the baby go, I began to understand then that there was something in me which knew far more than I did and which I could trust.

'In all that time, after the discovery of pregnancy till after the abortion, the only genuine feeling I had for myself was at that twelfth hour when I didn't want to lose that child. The rest was pressure, prejudice and opinion. My feeling was biological and instinctive, not linked with social consequences. I haven't a clue whether I could have coped if I hadn't had the abortion or what, with the opportunity to think and talk, my decision might have been.'

Claire, whose second abortion at 22 had taken on nightmarish proportions, with a severe infection that kept her in the hospital for 12 days, also had strong feelings of personal failure afterwards.

'I felt very needy. Anthony was attentive but he was still going to college and I still couldn't tell anyone else what had happened. I felt it was some kind of failure to have got into that pickle in the first place and then not be adult enough to cope with a child. And *then*, on top of all that, the abortion itself had gone wrong. I dwelt on the fact that I might never be able to have a child, although I knew it wasn't certain. (I have never felt able to tell my parents about either abortion and I know they would love grandchildren.)'

Claire became so upset and depressed that she decided to leave college. 'I hadn't been happy there. I had gone there to please my parents. I was saying, in effect, "I don't want the life that you, my parents, want for me. I don't want to teach."

'The abortion was a trigger for a lot of self-questioning. I regretted the abortion. I felt I had actually killed something and the difference this time was that what I had killed had been conceived in love.

'I was finding it impossible to talk about anything at that stage. I knew I had power and yet I felt powerless in my life. I felt I was of no personal worth, that I had no talent and my main function was just to support people who did.' Claire had planned, when she finished college, to get a job and support Anthony through a higher degree. In the event, the money Claire earned was not enough to support Anthony without a grant of his own and he was obliged to give up studying and get a job. A few months later he walked out of it and had a 'sort of breakdown' through which Claire looked after him.

She said: 'When I was 26 or 27, I felt physically and emotionally, for the first time, that I *did* want a child and that was when our relationship broke up because I realised I couldn't trust Anthony to support me. I didn't fall out of love with him. I wanted him to be manly and take some responsibility or get out. He waited for me to snap out of it and carry on supporting him, while he decided what to do with his life. That was it.

'I knew he couldn't support me as a wife, a lover and a mother. I think, in fact, I had made *him* my child. He had become far more childlike after the second abortion and I had encouraged that.'

Today Claire is 33 and not in a permanent relationship. Her insights into herself and the experience of abortion came a few years later, when she first started therapy (see Chapter 6). She recognised then, for the first time, that she was still grieving for that child.

'It is only sometimes now that I wish I had done differently. I think Anthony would have stuck with me. There are parts of him I miss, and that sense of life a child gives you — giving you your place in life. I know a young woman who is a single mother. Her life is hard and yet there is such a strong sense of life in her from her child. Sometimes for me life feels arid and barren.'

The gynaecologist Claire saw at the hospital for her second abortion had told her brusquely that she might not be able to carry a child again. 'I still fear that might be the case. Sometimes I think I couldn't bear being in a loving, caring, supportive relationship and not being able to have a child. That bit of fear stopped me, till recently, getting close in relationships. I find other people's pregnancies and babies difficult. I cannot get too close.

'Emotionally I regret the abortion. Logically, I don't. I still believe abortion is right for some people at some time because I've known people who had unwanted babies and resented them. And I've known people who *were* children who weren't wanted and that is absolute hell.'

Very many women say that they feel sad or envious around other people's children after an abortion. For some, like Claire, the feeling persists for years. Joanne, whose boyfriend Ben had not been able to entertain the idea of having their child and had also tried to put the abortion out of his mind, is another who still feels uncomfortable around children. She had her abortion at 22 and is now 25.

'I remember that, the day after my abortion, a friend rang and said, first thing, "Do you regret it?" I felt angry at her for that, it seemed so inappropriate. She then told me she was pregnant and said I could be the godmother to her baby. She kept writing to me and telling me her symptoms and I found it all very stabbing. I didn't want to replace my lost baby with hers. They would have been around the same age.

'I didn't want to be around children at all and I didn't know how to respond when people said they were pregnant. I just couldn't find it in me to say, "How nice!" I felt — and still feel — envious.'

Joanne is still in a relationship with Ben but it is one that is fraught with conflicting and unresolved feelings. 'I don't think I've ever been in love with him,' she admitted. 'To start with we were just friends and we should have left it that way. I don't see us staying together and yet I don't want to break it up.

'Why do I still see him? I feel emotionally connected to him because I have known him for four years and because of the abortion. And I think he feels connected to me in the same sort of guilty way too. It isn't positive, I know. I felt I drew apart from him after the abortion because I saw how different we were emotionally from each other.

'And yet I felt very possessive about him. I didn't want

him to have a relationship with someone else or have a baby with someone else. We moved in together, stupidly, trying to see if there was any point to our relationship, but I hardly spent any time there. I was still doing shift-work and sleeping some nights at my parents' house. We don't live together now.

'Now I don't mind if we eventually split up but I want *him* to meet someone before I do. I feel, if I met someone first, he wouldn't bother to keep in touch and he could forget all about the abortion. Whereas, the other way around, I feel he would feel he still had a responsibility towards me. So I could still ring him up, even if he had a girlfriend.'

She knows that part of her present need to 'hang on' is because she feels Ben has never properly acknowledged her pregnancy and abortion. 'I really feel I want him to *tell* someone about the baby. Then I wouldn't mind if he had a baby with someone else. But he told no one. There are pictures of me on our holiday in Derbyshire where I first discovered I was pregnant. I really like them, because I was pregnant. His friends were looking at them and said I seemed pale. I really wanted him to just come out and tell them *why*.

'I also have a fear that he wouldn't feel so bad about his friends knowing I had had an abortion, as long as they didn't know he was connected with it.'

There is, however, a part in Joanne herself which wants to deny the abortion ever happened. When she had a smear at a family planning clinic, she was asked if she had ever been pregnant, a routine question, and she quickly said no. In the new area where she is now living, she has not yet signed on with a general practitioner. 'That's because I dread having the abortion on my record. I think I might even deny it then too. I hate people making assumptions about me, about what it says if I have had an abortion. Ethically, for me, abortion has been the one thing in my life I'm not happy about.'

While Joanne prefers not to acknowledge that she has had a pregnancy that ended in abortion, she does, however, feel strongly positive about the pregnancy itself. It is the baby that she wants Ben to tell other people about, rather than the abortion, and she has similar wants for herself. 'A lot of my friends now have children,' she said. 'If someone is pregnant, I want so much to tell them I have been pregnant too.

'I *do* feel guilty. I feel, on the one hand, that there can never be a really good reason for having an abortion. And yet, I do also feel that those who disapprove, well, they have no right. They can't know what is happening in someone's life at the time. But, for me, abortion and my guilt have affected my attitude to my next pregnancy. Even if I knew I was having a handicapped child, I'd have to have it, because I couldn't have another abortion.'

Sarah also feels strongly that she would now take whatever life deals her. She had two abortions at a confused time in her life, after the death of her father, 12 years ago. She did not have strong conscious feelings about what she was doing at the time.

'After the second abortion, I was in a terrible mess. I didn't feel good but I don't recall feeling anything other than what a great nuisance it all was. Now I think my anger that my IUD had failed was arrogant,' she said. 'I thought in terms of choosing when *I* wanted a child and disregarded what my body was trying to tell me.

'I felt very anxious about contraception afterwards. I swore I would never have an abortion again, although I can't remember where the feeling came from. I think I felt I was damaging myself. I must have felt it on the physical level but, on a deeper level, I must have known it wasn't right spiritually either. I have been extremely conscientious about contraception since.' Between then and now, Sarah has had years of therapy, both individual and group work.

'I think there is a deeper meaning to what happens to us in life,' she says. 'I don't mean God but something to do with a kind of force of regeneration in life which I feel should be respected.

'Regret? It is hard to say. Probably yes because I feel that I spent a lot of time catching up on my relationship to life which could have happened earlier. That would have been inevitable if I had had a baby to bring up on my own. Or I would have responded to a miscarriage/abortion as a loss instead of a convenience.'

Sarah is now in an important and committed relationship, which began only recently, but feels, 'in a way, tainted'. She told her partner about the abortions only when she had agreed to be interviewed for this book. 'But I felt shame. I didn't really want to involve him in something I saw as sordid in my life.

'I know if I couldn't get pregnant now, I would feel very regretful. But I think I deserve it for assuming I could have children whenever I wanted. I think I will have been taught a hard lesson.'

The words as they appear on these pages make Sarah seem extremely self-castigating. In fact, she is full of energy and enthusiasms, is very self-conscious in the best possible sense and believes in going fully with life. She accepts why she had the abortions. With hindsight, for her, however, they were choices made by someone unconnected to life and to feelings.

Catherine too feels she lacked courage in having an abortion, but she is not entirely regretful. She had the abortion at 35. She is now nearly 42 and has no child.

'I feel it is too late for regret now. But every time I see Princess Diana's eldest son, Prince William, I do feel sad. She was pregnant at the same time as I was. I think, yes, my child would have started school now too. Yes, I could have managed, with or without Nick. But I'm not tearful about it. I didn't have the guts, that's all.'

During the weekend on which Catherine had thought they were now making plans to keep the baby, Nick had turned round and said, 'I didn't say I'd have it'. Catherine arranged an abortion as soon as she was home in London. She didn't hear from Nick for a week. After it was over, when she was spending the evening with a supportive friend, Nick rang. The friend answered and said:

'Catherine can't speak to you now. She has just had an operation.'

'I didn't feel a lot when I heard he had rung,' said Catherine. 'I was too involved with what had happened to me. But Nick must have been shocked when he realised what had happened. He was shattered that he hadn't been around.

'At 9am the next morning he was ringing my doorbell. He had driven down from Manchester to London. I felt nothing when I saw him and had nothing to say to him. He was very nervous. I don't recall the conversation but I do recall feeling closer towards him as the day went on. It became obvious he wanted to stay the night.

'In bed, he broke down and cried. I felt only anger. I thought, "You cry your heart out because I've done all that. Now it's your turn. I'm glad you are upset." I didn't want to comfort him. I had had a week of horrors. He could have a night of them. And it was all too late anyway.

'He was drastic and desperate. He said, "Let's get married right away and next year you can have a baby." I said, no, we're not changing a thing. Let's see how we get on. I could have had him there and then in the registry office, he was so consumed with remorse. But he didn't ever follow it through. He never mentioned the idea again.'

But they did stay together for quite some time afterwards. 'His often saying we would have a child in a year's time kept me happy. It was a fool's paradise. I preferred still to carry on imagining it would be okay.' When she finally accepted, two years later, that it wouldn't be, she stopped seeing him.

Today she is at last in a strong and committed relationship. Her partner, Dale, already has teenage children by a previous marriage. Catherine is yet again in a dilemma about pregnancy — unsure whether she feels she is now too old to want to try or whether, with Dale's approval, just to go for it.

'I think it is this awful caution I've always had about everything,' she says. 'But nothing is ever perfect about the timing of children. I always seem to want it perfect, so now I'm thinking, "How would it be to be 50 and have, say, a seven-year-old child? How would Dale feel about launching into babies all over again, when I am not 100 per cent positive about it myself?" I suppose I want him to say, "Take the coil out". But that's cowardly. Or perhaps just to know he wanted a child with me strongly enough is all that I need.

'I don't feel changed by the abortion. In fact I'm very much still the person I was, which is why I had it. I think I've missed, and still miss, loads of things in life by being so unwilling to take risks. Having a baby on my own would have been a huge risk.

'But I do feel ashamed that I didn't have the guts to go through with it on my own. Other people try for pregnancies and fail or have babies in terrible circumstances.'

Like many others, for all her own sadness, she does not decry abortion. 'I certainly don't feel abortion is wrong. I don't think a child should be unwanted or even only half wanted. I have no idea, if I had had the baby, what the real consequences would have been.'

Catherine at no point suffered any deep depression. But Anna did, after deciding at 20 weeks to terminate her pregnancy with a baby discovered to have thalassaemia. She had to go into labour to give birth to the child, dead.

Her first abortion was seven years ago. 'I was very depressed and miserable for a long time,' she said. 'I cried all the time. I felt better for being able to tell close friends the truth — my in-laws were at first hurt that we hadn't confided in them beforehand what might happen — but to strangers enquiring about my pregnancy, I felt a need to claim miscarriage.

'My doctor gave me drugs for my depression but they made me feel even more like a zombie. When I stopped them after a month, I felt a bit better. My husband was good. We talked to each other about it a lot, more than to relatives or friends. It was our shared problem and it did bring us closer.

'I was depressed and away from work for two and a half months. When I did return, I lost my job. I suppose I still wasn't ready to go back, and when my employer made some remark about losing pay if I didn't fill in the right forms, I was so upset by the way he spoke (though he didn't mean any harm) that I walked out.

'At the time, suddenly every woman I saw seemed to be pregnant and every time I was in the supermarket I would hear the word "baby". I felt I had had such a rough deal. Others have babies with no problem and think nothing of it.

'I regretted not seeing the baby after it was born. I kept questioning what had happened to it and had a bit of a nightmarish session with myself over that.

'The second time it was slightly easier, because this time I was prepared for the possibility of another affected child, but it was still hard. I felt lonely. At least for the second termination the hospital made special arrangements for me, away from the new mothers.

'I pulled myself together quicker. I felt, if I wanted a healthy baby, I would have to keep on, although it was scary. The next time the baby was all right and it was unbelievable. But I was so very careful throughout the pregnancy! I took no risks at all and even kept well out of the vicinity of any smoker.

'Paul and I had decided that one healthy baby would be enough. But then our daughter started asking for a brother or sister and we had another try. Unsuccessful, of course. Even now, there is a part of me that yearns for another.

'I do feel guilty about the three terminations, even now. I feel very sad when I think of each individual situation and I still don't really know if I did the right thing. But, conversely, I am happy I had the choice to terminate and have one healthy child. Without that choice, I wouldn't have risked having children at all.'

Joan, who had had one handicapped child and decided to terminate a pregnancy with another (she had had one healthy child in between) feels she was unlucky but didn't get depressed. 'It probably sounds awful but I didn't feel as bad as I might have. We just seemed to be unlucky and it was just one more blow. My husband Steven took it worse than I did.

'I do find, though, that I'm neurotic about my one living child. I see danger everywhere — crossing roads, things like that — but I try not to let it show. I don't want more children. I am 37 now and my fear is that, a next time, the baby would have Downs Syndrome.' (Joan's first child had been born with a very rare enzyme disorder of which he died aged six; the second handicapped foetus had an equally rare chromosome disorder, not Downs. Downs is a particular risk of late pregnancy and, for Joan, two unlucky pregnancies might well have become three.)

'Steven and I both came separately to the conclusion that we didn't want more children and it was a relief when we discovered we were thinking the same thing. Steven has now had a vasectomy.

'I think it is hardest when it comes to special dates. It was hard for me on the date the baby should have been born and then at Christmas. I felt I should have been shopping for toys for her too. She was actually due on my living son's birthday, which doesn't make things easier. For his sake, things have to be normal.

'I feel guilty when I think about women who can't have children, while I had a termination. But knowing the child wouldn't have survived makes that easier. I do anyway feel it is very much the woman who should have the right to choose. It is particularly sad when women feel they have to have abortions for social reasons, but I do feel it is their right.'

Some women I spoke to did feel that there were important positive aspects to their experience of abortion. Gillian felt so, very strongly indeed, at the start. She was 19 at the time.

'I stayed with a friend the day after the abortion. I was still sort of feeling nothing,' she remembers. 'Then, the next day, as I walked home, I suddenly felt free and relieved and high and confident! I felt really good about myself. I had made a decision on my own for the first time in my life and gone through with it. I even felt physically well.

'At the back of my mind I was thinking, "I'm sure I'm supposed to be depressed but right now I want to be happy." I wanted to keep talking about how I was feeling because I felt so good about the changes in myself.

'I carried on living alone and, for the first time, I really did feel it was wonderful, instead of just pretending and feeling lonely. There was an inner strength that I had got in touch with. I joined a women's group and felt strongly about feminist issues. I even started arguing and discussing with lecturers instead of sitting mousy and quiet. It was a very good time.

'At the same time, I was pushing Rob away.' (It was Gillian who had resented the fact that Rob couldn't be the one to have the abortion.) 'He had no part in this new me. I said I didn't want sex with him any more because of the fear of pregnancy (I was still refusing contraception because I hadn't resolved the issues about responsibility) but I was actually becoming anti-man. I focused all that on him. I resented his freedom during the time of the abortion. I resented his being a man.

'Then I went abroad to study for a year and that sort of distorted the relationship because we met only if he came over for a holiday or vice versa and so we could idealise each other more when apart.'

It was on one of Rob's visits that Gillian became pregnant again, although they had not had full sex. All her bitterness against Rob returned full-blast.

'I felt so angry. All the good feelings about myself disappeared and I didn't have any good feelings about the pregnancy this time either. I felt the presence as evil. It is a year ago now and I am still working through what it was all about.'

She came back to England for the pregnancy test and the abortion. At the clinic she went to, she was offered the chance to return for follow-up counselling which she later took up, with far-reaching effects (see Chapter 6). The immediate aftermath of her abortion, however, was unexpected and terrifying and the tale is quite a long one.

'I remember lying in the room at the clinic staring out at a bright moonlit night and feeling so alone. Rob was sleeping outside in the car. I wished he was under a hedge! But he had been far more involved than last time. He arranged all the practicalities. I was on automatic and I don't think I could have coped. It was so painful that all this was happening again. So unfair. I kept thinking, why me?

'It took away all my confidence. I had seen that first pregnancy and abortion as a blow of fate and I had risen above it. Now, a second blow and I felt helpless again. (I now, although I didn't then, accept responsibility for that first pregnancy.)

'After the abortion I felt a really horrible burning pain and took the opportunity to have a good cry. But I didn't get as much attention as I wanted. I said I was crying because of the physical pain but really, I think, it was the mental torture that caused it.

'Before I had gone in, I had started bleeding and thought maybe it was a period after all, or a miscarriage. But the clinic just carried on anyway. I really would like to have known because it would have made me feel so much better if I hadn't been pregnant at all or had miscarried. But I didn't feel I was taking a life by abortion anyway. I hated what was in me this time so much that I wouldn't have cared.

'Because the abortion was done so early, I had to have another test a week later to check all was well. I had the test and it was positive! I felt so bad that I actually rang my mother and asked her to come to see me. It was quite brave of me to do that because we didn't talk much of emotional things. She liked to think of me as independent and here I was asking for help.

'She got in her car and drove three hours to be with me. But, once together, we still didn't show any emotion. No tears, no hugs. We played the game of my avoiding responsibility and her colluding with me. We blamed the doctors for what had happened and had a more comfortable solidarity on that.

'She and Rob both came back with me to the clinic for another test and this time it was negative. I was so confused. I wasn't sure if perhaps I had never been pregnant — or that perhaps I still was. I just couldn't cope. I got so depressed, packed up my studies abroad for the rest of the year, dropped out of the exams and decided to stay at home with my parents.

'I remained unsure for the next three or four months whether I was pregnant or not. I was never free of the fear of it, unlike the first time. If I had any pains, I instantly associated them with pregnancy. I felt scared of everything and lacked confidence. I didn't trust anything at all — I even expected cars and vacuum cleaners to blow up.

'I also felt I couldn't talk to any friends about this abortion because they would have lost all sympathy for me this time round. I didn't think I deserved sympathy either. I had terrible dreams and would wake up frightened. I was weepy all the time and frightened of a breakdown. I spent the entire summer holidays just hanging around, doing nothing. It's a blur.

'When I started back to college, in England, in September that year, I came back to live in London and felt better away from my parents' home. I met a girl at college and we started a relationship together. I felt *that* would take me away from Rob.

'He gave me fireworks. He didn't understand what I was doing and I didn't either. But the relationship felt right for me. Carol would hold me when I cried and helped me get through the bad patches. I fear now I used her for that. She was the one person I had needed all along — someone who would listen and let me cry.'

By this time, Gillian had been back for post-abortion counselling and had started having regular counselling sessions at an advice centre for under 25s. It was after many such sessions that she started to understand the predicaments in her life, that had led to pregnancy, and how to move on.

Andrea had felt utterly decisive about needing an abortion because the baby she found she was carrying was, like Gillian's second, an 'evil presence' to her. She says she never gave the abortion another thought after it was over. However, a year afterwards, the man with whom she had had a passionate on-off relationship for years (not the father of the baby) came back into her life. She was not using the pill, because she had developed a reaction to it, and was simply trying to stick to the safe time of the month method.

'I knew I didn't mind if I got pregnant,' she said. 'And when I did get pregnant, I felt wonderful. I told Joe and he said get rid of it and I said get lost. Joe even fixed me an appointment for an abortion and I was sort of going along with it, but I knew in my heart I would be having the baby. And that Joe wouldn't be with me. My mother was behind me and all my friends, so I felt prepared to have it on my own.

'This time I felt I had something live and wonderful inside me within days. I still don't know why I felt so differently the first time. The first time I had made arrangements to be away on work abroad which would all have had to be cancelled if I had stayed pregnant and I didn't want to cancel them. But the second time, if I had had those same arrangements made, I'd have cancelled them without a moment's thought.

'Joe stopped seeing me when he knew I was keeping the baby — and I knew that was what he would do. I was absolutely devastated when, at 13 weeks, I lost it. In the hospital, I lay in my bed feeling totally destroyed, whereas the first time I was up and out of bed and back to my life. I grieved for a very long time. The early weeks were terrible but my mother, I remember, was very supportive.

'It took me two years to get over the trauma. It never occurred to me that the abortion had any bearing on the miscarriage and I don't think it did. I stayed in and hardly saw friends till, two years later, a woman friend persuaded me to go out with her and I met a man who made me laugh.

'For three or four months we had such fun. He was married with children. And he was ugly. I wanted to see a photo of his children and when I saw that they were gorgeous I thought, well, if I do get pregnant, I'll have a nice-looking child.

'I told him I was not on the pill and that if I did get pregnant I would not get rid of it. He said fine but he would have nothing to do with it. And that was also fine by me. He doesn't actually live in England and was only here for a while.'

Andrea, at 42, now has a five-year-old son whom she adores. 'He may have a single parent but he has given me so much confidence and his teacher says he is one of the most well-adjusted and happy children in his school. In a way I think everything has worked out for the best. Although I still regret the loss the miscarriage brought me, I think Joe might have made things difficult for me if that baby had been born.

'And the first I regret not at all. I have never had views on abortion beyond feeling it is up to the individual always.'

Maria feels sadness that she didn't have the courage to go ahead and have her child but no actual regret that she had an abortion in the end. She and Stuart had changed their minds about going ahead with the unplanned pregnancy when the fear and anxiety they were each feeling started driving them apart. Maria had filled over 50 pages of a notebook while in the clinic on the night after her abortion, recording all the events that occurred from pregnancy to abortion and her feelings about them.

'I am glad I have that record. It is upsetting to read but what I wanted was to make sure that I didn't look back long after with rosier spectacles and think, "It wasn't that bad. Why didn't I go through with it?" For me at the time, the stress, the uncertainty about whether I wanted to change my life so dramatically to include a baby, and the anxiety about whether Stuart and I could stay together through it all, or lose our love, were almost overwhelming.

'I know why I had that abortion. I know myself well

enough to know that, although indeed I might have coped, I would not suddenly have done an about-face and become positive, serene and glowing. It was quite humbling to learn that I didn't have the automatic capacity to adjust and make the best of things, as perhaps I tend to expect: that, when something serious happens, I won't necessarily be able to rise determinedly to the occasion.

'I think about the baby that could have been, sometimes. On what might have been its birthday and on anniversaries of the abortion. That was now three years ago and I am 37.

'Stuart did stick by me, very much so and very lovingly, afterwards. Two years later we married. I can't say that the experience itself brought us closer together but it tested us. And it has not been without its adverse effects on our life, I think. We had always had a very passionate sex life. I had the IUD fitted and I think there was a part of me that then felt very disconnected from any biological function. I did have, briefly, after the abortion, a yearning instantly to try for a baby — like a sort of atonement. Once the IUD was in, that ceased to be in question.

'Somewhere along the way, I lost a lot of interest in sex. I can't say that that is directly linked to the abortion because we have had lots of turbulent times in our relationship, due to other things, that made both of us feel insecure. And the effect of that, on my part, was that I was less willing to be open and vulnerable sexually. But, one night, I allowed myself to say to him during sex, "I want a baby" and the positive effect on me sexually was extremely strong.

'However, I'm not at all sure that wasn't a bit romantic, an exciting bit of risk-taking without the real risk.'

Now, as regards having children, like Catherine she feels cautious. 'We got married because we started talking about children again,' she said. 'But part of me feels, "Do I really want to start now?" I'd be nearly 39 even if I was successful straightaway. And the selfish part of me isn't sure I'm prepared to change my life so profoundly for the next 18 or so years. The other part of me feels I would be a good mother and that I will miss out on something good for both me and a baby, and for Stuart's and my relationship, if we don't.

'For me, there is another thing too. Because of having had one abortion — of a pregnancy that arose because of my overwhelming romantic feelings towards Stuart at the time and the desire to have our child — I am reluctant to get pregnant again under any romantic illusion. I think with pleasure of a baby that looks like me and like him and the fun we would have with a young one. But the realities are also sleepless nights, anxiety, schooling and adolescent rebellion. I have to be sure I am ready to embrace it all — and yet, how can one be sure? Isn't it always a risk and one you just have to get on with, in the end?'

For Diana, the depression she experienced after abortion was not a matter of whether she would ever have a child — she already had three — but confronting the fact she was approaching middle-age and the significance of this was that she *knew* she would never have another. She was 41.

'Even though it was my choice to have an abortion — I couldn't have coped with two teenagers, a two-year-old and a new baby — I felt very much the onrush of middle age, signified by no more babies and the approaching menopause. I had been only 10 weeks' pregnant but I put on a lot of weight very quickly and was left with a very strange and middle-aged shape which didn't help matters. It took a time to get rid of, unlike after the other pregnancies.

'I felt okay about the abortion itself. I have always felt fine about it up to 13 weeks. After 16 weeks, I feel the baby is more real and, for me, it would be murder. Everyone has their own personal limits in this area and these happen to be mine, that's all.

'But there was a little bit of me that would have loved a little girl. I have three sons. I know you can't dictate to nature but I did have to reconcile myself to never having a daughter. I had desperately wanted a girl when Will, our two-year-old, was born. It was fortunate I knew his sex at 20 weeks, after amniocentesis, so I had time to get used to it.

'All of these feelings were coloured by fatigue and by the fact that my hormones were in upheaval. I'm sure my ovaries were in decline ever since Will was born, as I had increasingly had bouts of depression. Since going on hormone replacement therapy, I have felt a million times better.

'Three years on, I feel I have calmed down in my life. I have achieved most of my ambitions and I would now like to be able to work less and do more of what I want to do. I have always loved singing and would love to give more time to that, perhaps join a choir.

'I am sad Len will not have another child, especially as he too yearned for a daughter. But it has been the right thing for me. I think I've always been an extremely conscientious mother. Now is the time to think of myself.'

Joyce, who was 39 and the mother of a 19-year-old son when she fell pregnant after her sterilisation failure, never felt any sadness about the fact that she would not have any more children. She had already confronted and chosen that when she opted for sterilisation in the first place. But, having been the victim of misfortune, and unwillingly pregnant again, she still remained untouched emotionally by the thought of children.

'Prior to having the abortion done, I had come into contact with an unusually large number of babies. It was nearly Christmas and, at the shoe shop where I am manageress, there was a Christmas party to which the young women came with their babies and toddlers. But I experienced no overwhelming maternal instinct whatsoever.'

Joyce's big dilemma was that she was not in favour of abortion, particularly for herself, and yet she did not want to give birth to her child. 'What I did feel afterwards, the abortion having been done at five months, was a terrible fear that the baby had been born alive and screaming. Two weeks afterwards I cried and cried about that and all my pain and anxiety came out with Richard (her husband). Had we done the right thing? All that. I felt as if I was back in my glass case, isolated from the world. I was accepting that I was talking about "our child". Had "our child" suffered? I have to find out, in fact. I shall ask the doctor when he does my next sterilisation. I don't know how I'll handle it if it wasn't born dead but I have to *know*.' (The abortion had taken place only a month before the interview for this book.)

Joyce also felt that she wanted to know whether the baby was a boy or a girl, and she plans to find that out too. She had tried to find out at the scan before the abortion, but the signs were not conclusive. 'I don't know why I feel I want to know but I do,' she said.

For all that her own experience of the abortion clinic was, to her, appalling and devoid of human comfort from the staff, she does feel that there have been unanticipated and very positive effects on her relationship with second husband Richard, aged 30 and nine years her junior.

'Richard and I had been going through a difficult year. I feel that all this, the pregnancy and the abortion, has thrown our relationship up in the air and made it come down differently. It brought us closer together because it is something very much of our own. Family don't know about it. And, more especially, it was the first time I have felt totally emotionally dependent on Richard.

'I have always been very independent. I had to be, as a single parent for so long. This independence was compounded by the fact that Richard has been very haphazard about work, starting jobs and leaving them and being out of work for a while. I never felt able to lean on him totally, even if I had wanted to.

'Then this happened and in some way it helped. I found that he *could* be there when I needed him. And it showed him that I could be vulnerable and not always so in control. I had never shown him that before. I think it has been good for him to feel needed. He was able to cut out the "that's our child" part and focus on "she needs me". If he had focused on the child, even though he didn't want one either, he might have missed out on my need for support.

'He has told me that, on the day of the operation, he

realised how much he had let me down, being in and out of work and telling me lies and leaving me to shoulder any financial burdens. He is in a job that interests him and is really planning to stick with it now.

'I said to him just recently, "If something bad happens, some good must come out of it, otherwise there has been no purpose". I feel we have to make something good come out of that abortion and that means our relationship must get better. It has got to mean something. Losing that child's life has got to have created something, otherwise it was all bad. And I do feel already so much more secure in my marrige.

'I still don't agree with abortion. It is literally playing God with a life and that is why I'm so against it. But I don't believe you should have a child you don't want either.'

These seem impossibly contradictory feelings to reconcile. Yet such feelings, each felt equally strongly, are familiar to so very many women who have faced abortion.

6.
SHARING
The need for more help

The freedom to talk about the experience of abortion and
the complicated feelings it arouses is often a vital factor in
emotional healing. Anxieties or negative feelings which
remain locked inside can easily get out of proportion. Not
every woman experiences strong and difficult feelings
which she needs to express, but many are taken unawares
by the power of their emotions. If an unresolved, and often
unrecognised, conflict led to the pregnancy in the first
place, this too is likely to seethe on under the surface at a
time when a woman is more emotionally vulnerable than
usual.

Counselling services commonly report being contacted
by women whose abortion took place as long as 20 years
ago. Many had never dared speak out before, and many
had only just realised that such services exist, offering the
opportunity to share feelings which have not diminished
with time but may have become an increasing burden to
bear. Others only realise many years on that abortion *was* a
significant event in their lives, yet one that was given no
importance at the time by them or others.

Grace, who had the illegal abortion, very much wishes
that she had had someone to confide in or to advise her at
the time. She mourned her loss, alone, for four or five
years, during which time she married and had a child.

It was the stigma, the social and parental disapproval,
that stopped Grace speaking out, over 30 years ago. For
Claire, 10 years ago at the age of 22, it was a personal
sense of failure that kept her silent. Her husband Anthony
was attentive but, as his keenness to carry on at college

with her financial support had been one reason for the abortion, she could not share her grief with him without appearing accusatory. She suppressed it but was depressed for a long time.

However, it was *after* she had apparently got her life back together and found a job she liked that she realised for the first time the extent of her grief and that it was still very much with her.

'It was seven years ago,' she said, 'when I went to a psychodrama workshop' (a form of therapy that focuses on playing out emotionally important scenarios from one's life). 'We were given a pillow and told to make it be something that meant something to us. I made mine the child I had lost. It just happened, without my consciously deciding to do it. I cried my eyes out. That was when I started to allow myself to grieve.'

The workshop was Claire's first experience of therapy. She decided to find a form of psychotherapy that she could commit herself to, on a regular weekly basis, to explore all the confusion and suppressed feelings she now realised were inside her. During the process, she was divorced from Anthony.

'It wasn't counselling for the abortion I needed,' she said. 'It was counselling about my life in general. I was doing things and making decisions without really knowing much about who I really was or what I wanted. Getting pregnant and having the abortion was part of that.'

Since therapy, she has come to realise how little she felt she had the right to have feelings at all. She had tended to go along with what people who were important to her, such as her parents, had wanted for her, and she had never felt she could complain. She now accepts that she too has needs, that she too wants support, which Anthony could never offer. She has also recognised her difficulties in accepting herself as a sexual woman.

'I think,' she said, 'that I saw abortion as confirmation that I was being punished for not being a proper woman. Proper women have babies, whereas I had been told, after the abortion, that I might never now be able to have them.

'I am aware, too, of how I have avoided close relationships that might lead me to have to face, in reality, that I might not ever have a baby. I have tended to go for much younger men, so that there was less likelihood of anything serious developing.

'I had buried my feelings about the abortions so deeply that it took a long time for them to come up. But I now feel sure the feelings were affecting my life and my relationships. It is only very recently that I have let myself get close to a man of around my own age and it feels scary but good.'

Apart from Andrea, who had deliberately not talked about her pregnancy before or after but just got on with getting an abortion, only Grace and Claire, of the women who spoke to me, had not talked to a single sympathetic person at the time. Of the rest, a few felt that the help they had received from friends or from their partners had been sufficient for them to come to terms with what had happened and to carry on with their lives normally afterwards.

Joan, who had had one handicapped child and terminated a pregnancy in which she was carrying another, said: 'My husband was very good and so was my health visitor and GP. But I had no real follow-up as such. I did talk to friends in the group I belong to (a parent support group for those with children suffering the rare condition that killed her first son) and that was a therapy in itself. I never felt I needed professional counselling.'

Neither did Catherine, whose pregnancy at 35 was very much wanted by her but not, unfortunately, by her boyfriend Nick. 'I do feel I wish I could have had counselling *before* the abortion but not afterwards. It was all too late then.

'I received support from friends before the abortion and that was important. But afterwards I didn't talk even to them much about the actual experience. It was such a horrible day that it is not something I wanted to talk about. And I certainly didn't want any support from Nick. But I don't feel I've suppressed anything. I am sad about what happened and I do think about it sometimes. I don't push the abortion away and pretend it never happened. But I don't feel changed by it or that it has had some subtle unconscious effect on my life.'

Joyce, who had a pregnancy after sterilisation and an abortion at five months, greatly values the support she can draw on from her husband Richard. 'Two weeks after the abortion, I had a terrible Sunday, when I was in floods of tears about whether the baby had been born screaming and worrying whether we had done the right thing after all. It all came out with Richard and he was marvellous.

'If I ever feel like that again, it is Richard I would choose to be with. I wouldn't feel the need of any professional counselling.

'I feel Richard has really taken his share in all this. He asked me recently when I was having my second sterilisation done. I said to him, "Why don't *you* have a vasectomy instead?" I was just testing him, really. I thought he'd say an instant macho no, but in fact he said that he would, if I really wanted him to.

'I wouldn't have dreamt of letting him have it. I am 39, have a 19-year-old son and I know I don't want another child. Richard is only 30. If we split up or something happened to me, how might a second wife feel if she couldn't have childen with him, if that was what they wanted? But his saying what he did made me feel cared for. It was important.'

Diana, 41 at the time of her abortion and the mother of three boys, did not have any post-abortion counselling. She was very clear in her decision to have an abortion, with no doubts or reservations. But other concerns about her life at the time meant she might have welcomed some kind of support group.

'I'm not sure that I did need to talk to anyone else about the abortion itself, beyond my husband Len. But what I did need to work on more were the reasons leading up to my getting pregnant again in the first place. I had started being less careful about using the diaphragm and there was something behind that.

'A shoulder to cry on that wasn't Len's might have been useful, to help me explore that. If someone had suggested a group at the time, it might well have been brilliant.'

Others very firmly feel that post-abortion groups or therapy of a general kind had a very important impact on how they have since made sense of their lives.

Joanne, who resents her boyfriend Ben's failure openly to acknowledge her pregnancy and abortion, replied to an advertisement seeking women who had had abortions and who would be willing to learn how to run a Samaritan-type service for others.

'We were selected by a long interview and then trained by a marriage counsellor. The idea was to offer a phone listening service so that women who had strong feelings about their abortion but no one to tell could ring in.

'At the time I applied, I thought I was okay with my own feelings because I had talked to friends. But the course was so good because, in doing it, we were made to think about our own abortions in a deeper way. It was on the course that we were asked what we thought was the reason *why* we had got pregnant when we did. I had never thought about it like that before.

'That was when I came to realise that what I had been most in need of, at the time, was a home. Somewhere I could feel settled. In my unconscious mind, I suppose, having a baby seemed as if it could offer me that. But it was very unlikely, in actual fact, as I didn't have a home of my own, I was doing shift-work and my boyfriend wouldn't countenance a baby. I didn't really want a baby at that time nor do I think I really wanted one with Ben. I don't trust our being parents together.

'A few months after my abortion, I changed my job. Now I don't do shift-work. And I moved into a flat I share with two other women. That part has been very positive indeed. I really hate the fact that I have had an abortion, but it hasn't crippled me. It hasn't made me more insecure, more depressed or less capable. At the group it was good to be with other women in my position. There was no need to feel defensive, for once.

'I also realise I'm not all sorted out yet. There are feelings, about the abortion and about Ben, that I need to work on and resolve. I still tend to want to blame *him* for the abortion. I want it to be more his fault than my own and I even try to make it appear that way to myself.'

Sarah started individual and group therapy about a year after her abortion but the decision was not directly connected with that. A friend had joined a group and Sarah grew interested.

Several years of therapy have been a revelation to her. She has changed from being someone she saw as unconscious of the causes and effects of her actions into someone who is in touch with her own feelings and intuitive about others. She is extremely critical of her old self, who took the consequences of abortion too lightly, but she has also learned from it and now makes everything she can of whatever life offers.

'I certainly take abortion much more seriously now. I would never have one again, whatever the circumstances. Since therapy, and since knowing couples who can't conceive, I feel it is wrong to tamper with life in that way. What I feel is not about killing babies, but that conception and birth are miracles and have a meaning beyond anything we necessarily know about. I may not know why I conceive or can't conceive but I no longer accept it is a purely mechanical event. There is greater meaning to it than that.

'I don't feel my ego, my decision-making powers and my ability to tamper (through abortion) should be the ruling forces over a deeper instinct. Since therapy, I have more sense of humility about all kinds of things; about illness, about death, about life.

'Before, with the abortion, I didn't use what life sent me in the right way. Difficult things in life are challenges to which there are many ways we can respond. I am in a very committed relationship with someone now but it so nearly didn't happen because of certain difficult circumstances for us both. It would have been easier to opt out. Instead, I faced it as a challenge and with help I found the courage to go ahead.

'If I cannot have children now, it will be a hard lesson and deserved for assuming that I would have them only when it suited me, and for not making them precious enough.'

Maria was having therapy sessions at the time of her abortion. It was she who was grateful for having been made to feel all her buried feelings about what she was doing, instead of pushing them down to deaden herself against pain. She and Stuart had at first planned to have their baby, then found they couldn't cope with their mixed feelings.

'I did get a lot of help from talking about the abortion,' she said. 'The morning I came home, I went almost immediately to visit a friend who had also had an abortion and who knew the whole story of what had happened with me. I was feeling pure relief at the time and she understood that and I was glad to be able to express it without feeling guilty.

'When I saw Stuart, I told him that I had written over 50 pages about what had happened, and my feelings, while at the clinic. He asked if I would read it to him. It was a very honest account of how I felt about him and about myself in all this, and I felt a bit anxious about reading it out loud. But I also wanted to. And I was glad I did. He listened in absolute silence and with great sadness of his own and it brought us very close together.

'My own sadness all came out when I went to my therapy group. It was all women and, when I had seen them last, they had been congratulating me on my pregnancy. I was very fearful about explaining what had happened. I thought I would be judged and criticised. I remember crying a lot while talking.

'In fact, they were wonderful. One woman whose tongue I had particularly feared was the first to speak afterwards and she said, with a great deal of feeling, "I think you have been so brave". I felt so grateful to her and so supported. There was a lot of sadness in the room. It made me realise

I could express my own pain about what had happened to me without being defensive. I didn't have to heap on the horrors or try to escape the responsibility for the decision just to get sympathy. Nor did I have to pretend I was okay to justify that my decision was the right one.

'I made the decision of abortion. I made it with much pain and there is the pain of loss that follows. The fact I "chose" that loss didn't deny me the right to my sadness in that room. It was a relief to find that all my conflicting feelings could be accepted.

'I still think, though, that if I hadn't been made to confront myself and accept all those conflicting feelings *before* the abortion, I would have found it harder to allow myself to have them afterwards. As it was, I think I was able to go forward again and feel good about other things in my life quite quickly.'

Counselling had an extremely significant effect on Gillian's life, dramatically changing the way she lives and her ambitions. Although abortion is not the catalyst that anyone would choose, the sense Gillian has made of the experience, and the actions she has taken, can be described as nothing other than highly positive and productive. Her story reads almost like a happy ending to a novel, except that she now has far too much self-awareness to assume that she has her life all sorted out. The story strikes, however, a particularly uplifting note on which to end this chapter.

After her first abortion, she had felt unexpectedly very strong and effective, having made her first ever real decision in life. Then she was shocked to find she was pregnant again, without even having had full sex. A check-test after the second abortion came up positive and then, a week later, negative, and the whole confusing scenario destroyed her fragile newly-found confidence in life. Her enormous resentment that her boyfriend Rob wasn't obliged to go through abortion came surging back and she started a relationship with a woman.

'I was in a terrible mess, really,' she said. 'Carol used to hold me when I cried and that was what I had needed all along — someone just to listen and sympathise. I feel bad now that I might have used her just for that.

'I decided I needed help and went for counselling at a centre for under 25s. The counsellor challenged me about my feelings towards my mother. I thought my mother was perfect at that time and I was trying to live up to her ideals for me, of being an independent career woman rather than a mother stuck with five children, like her. I started to realise for the first time that her ideals weren't mine. And that I had resented her for her lack of comfort and emotional contact during my life.

'The counsellor also asked me *why* I got pregnant and that made me feel awful. I had always somehow avoided taking any responsibility for it at all and just blamed Rob. But then I started to think about it.

'I had stopped using the pill because my mother said it was dangerous but she hadn't suggested any alternative. I hadn't realised till then just how much influence she had over me. I had abdicated all responsibility for myself. *I* never tried to find an alternative. I think now there were a lot of things going on. I was looking for attention. I think I felt a baby would love me and could compensate for the lack of loving contact with my mother. And I was in unconscious conflict about living her ideals which weren't my own.

'Once I started taking on responsibility for the first pregnancy, I felt such relief! At around the same time Rob, who had taken all the blame I'd thrown at him, suddenly wrote to me to say I *did* have some responsibility for what had happened. I was so glad to see that letter.

'But I remember too feeling worried about the apparent power of my subconscious. All these things had been driving me and I hadn't known. I told the counsellor that and she told me to make space for myself to think and get in touch with what motivates me. (I had always been so busy keeping busy and not really thinking at all.) That is a part of my life now. I keep a diary and I question *why* things happen.

'I'm kinder to myself too and that was another of the

counsellor's suggestions. She said I had been hurting myself a lot and didn't treat myself enough.

'But one of the *most* important things to come out of the counselling was that I realised I was not happy on my own. I slowly started to accept my vulnerabilities and needs. The strong independent me wasn't me at all. I think I'd even seen Rob as a weakness of mine — my mother had said don't marry and get tied down and so I had had to keep trying to push him away.

'All this took months, once a week, and it took an even longer time to get into my head. But I was feeling very powerful about the very fact that I had gone to counselling. I had done something to get my life in order. I also felt good because I did well in my college exams.

'But there was a bad patch after leaving college. I was still with Carol but I had stopped the counselling sessions. I was starting to push things away again. Rob was phoning me three times a week, asking me back, and I hated seeing that neediness in him and was distant. What I didn't realise fully was the neediness in myself and that I also wanted him.

'Rob gave up his job as a librarian and went to work in Germany for a few months. That gave me time to think. I kept feeling, "I do love him" but I fought that feeling because I disliked the idea of going back to him. Then the stage came when I couldn't fight it any longer. I was unhappy because I wasn't accepting what I wanted. I was being distant from Carol and she was upset. Eventually I decided to try and get Rob back and split up with Carol.

'I felt I had forgiven him completely and that was such a relief. And, of course, it wasn't him I had forgiven but myself. It was also a relief to accept that I wanted and needed him.

'For the first time ever, I started challenging my mother. I told her I was cross that she didn't realise my exam results were a real achievement for me — she had wanted me to get a first, so the next thing down wasn't good enough. And I rejected a job she had half managed to line up for me, in advertising. I wanted to do something entirely different and not half so high-powered.

'When Rob came back from Germany, I told him I wanted him back. But I think he has realised he doesn't want me back as much as he thought while I want him more than I'd thought! We are seeing how it goes.

'We use condoms now. The weird thing is my period was late again recently and I felt totally differently. I felt I *could* have a baby if it happened. To allow that feeling was uplifting. In a way I was disappointed when my period came. Rob and I have talked about it, fantasising a pregnancy. He loves children. It was wonderful to think it could be a possibility instead of an instant negative.

'It was almost a luxurious feeling — like maternal feelings I have suppressed and not allowed myself to feel. It's luxurious to feel the depth of them and sense they are sincere and genuine. I do think I would like a child. I would never say abortion is out but I'm more likely to want a child. I feel that now, in fact, I could handle an abortion but I'd be more prepared to put my energy into a child than into an abortion.

'I think of showing my mother "my child". She would probably hate it. If she did, I would consider it a rejection of me. I don't think she even now realises how much I have changed.

'I still feel negative unresolved feelings about my second abortion but I don't force myself to try to sort them out. There's a danger of trying too hard to make sense of one's life by fitting bits together like a jigsaw puzzle. It is enough that I feel I have people now I can talk to. I was never able to talk much about anything before.

'Abortion certainly led me to face myself and my illusions. But I don't feel I'm suddenly all sorted out. I'm only 22. There will be many more crossroads and changes in my life yet.'

7.
REVIEWING
Abortion as two therapists see it

It is neither possible nor desirable to generalise about the experience of abortion. Women vary in their attitudes towards it, their personal experience of it, and their feelings about it both before and after. But it can help very much to know that any or all of a whole range of reactions are natural and normal and, by sharing in the feelings of others, it is possible to feel less alone with one's own.

I spoke to two psychotherapists who have spent many years helping hundreds of women to cope with the experience of abortion. Theirs is as broad a view of the emotional aspects of abortion as it is perhaps possible to acquire and I am grateful to them for sharing their empathy and insights. Their approach to abortion counselling is a product of who they are as individuals, and as therapists, and of the experience they have gained. They are not necessarily representative of abortion counsellors in general.

Gillian Isaacs Hemmings is a psychotherapist in private practice who has also been associated with the Marie Stopes clinic in London for the past five years, first as a pre-abortion counsellor and later also as a post-abortion counsellor. Mira Dana has been running post-abortion groups at the Women's Therapy Centre, in London and elsewhere, for the last eight years. Both feel strongly that supporting 'a woman's right to choose' should not mean having to deny that the choice is painful.

'We can't avoid pain when we all have feelings,' said

Gillian, 'and we can't by-pass those feelings and hope to heal. There is inevitably pain in the process of healing and I don't think there is any woman who doesn't need some sort of help after an abortion, whether it is from a supportive partner, family or friend or from a counsellor.

'Because of social disapproval and women's own mixed feelings, abortion tends not to be discussed enough, before or after. With the time element working against them, a lot of women feel they have to rush into a decision — and, of course, at times, they do have to. But it is a pity because, in a pregnancy that is confirmed early, it is good to give yourself time to experience your experience as having a beginning, a middle and an end. Even if a woman thinks she is sure of what she is doing, it isn't a good thing to say yes to a bed if it is offered for the next day. It is too soon to assimilate what is happening.

'In Britain, abortion is not on demand and women tend to be in a panic, fearing they will be turned down. They expect *not* to be sympathised with, so they come prepared with a full-of-impact story to convince a doctor or counsellor of their case.

'A woman may even come straight in and say, "I will kill myself if I don't get an abortion" because she fears that any other feelings won't be seen as valid. But that means she doesn't give herself the space to look at *all* that she is feeling. For instance, she might feel, "I think I want an abortion but I'm not totally sure," or "I don't want a child, yet I felt, thank God I'm fertile!" Or "I did feel good at first, for a while."

'If she doesn't feel free to express those sorts of mixed feelings, a lot of important personal work in coming to terms with abortion — or continuing a pregnancy — doesn't get done.'

Both Gillian and Mira encourage women to acknowledge all these kinds of conflicting feelings. Some may be immediately apparent to the woman herself, others not.

'Being pregnant and terminating the pregnancy is itself an expression of conflict,' said Gillian. 'It is like going in one direction and then dramatically changing to another, so it is unusual not to have mixed feelings. It is rare, in my experience, for women not to have some good feelings about pregnancy at first.

'Much of the conflict, however, may not be conscious. It is about wanting something and not being able to have it. Contraception of course is by no means 100 per cent perfect but a large percentage of the women I see don't have straightforward contraceptive failures. They forget the pill or the diaphragm because something else is going on that isn't conscious.'

For a woman who gets pregnant accidentally when her children are all grown up and she can at last go to work, the unconscious conflict may be that she is unsure of her new role and doesn't quite trust her creative abilities outside the family — although, consciously, she is dying to get a job. A similar confusion about role and lack of confidence may lead to unplanned pregnancy in the young girl who has just passed her exams and is set for college.

Failing relationships may be brought sharply into focus and 'tested' by an unexpected pregnancy. Or conception may occur on the anniversary of the death of someone dear or influential in one's life, like a mother or father. And unresolved feelings about one's own mother may very often come into the picture — a need for approval by having a baby, like she did, or to separate from her and the perhaps suffocating mother-figure she represents by getting pregnant and not keeping the baby.

'Very commonly, someone who *needs* care gets pregnant,' said Gillian. 'One young girl became pregnant after her parents split up and she went to live with an aunt. *She* felt like an aborted baby. Also, career women who are terribly busy and giving all their time to others may get pregnant, unconsciously, as a way to stop that. They may be carrying a baby but they identify with it themselves. They are the ones who are wanting to feel looked after.'

Testing fertility is sometimes at the heart of an unplanned pregnancy, in younger childless women and in older ones whose families have grown up. 'I found a series of women,' said Gillian, 'who had had their families and so their husbands had a vasectomy. The women had one-night stands and became pregnant. It seemed to me that they needed to know that they could still conceive. I put that to them and they all said yes!'

Mira believes that getting pregnant and having an abortion can, unconsciously, be one united action. 'Unconsciously the getting pregnant and the abortion have a function in the woman's life.'

In *Living with the Sphinx* (The Woman's Press, £5.95), a selection of papers from the Women's Therapy Centre, including one she wrote herself called 'Abortion — the Right to Feel', Mira explains this idea further:

'I believe that for some women getting pregnant and having an abortion is one joint experience. If such a woman were asked what she would do in the event of becoming pregnant, she would know more or less what she would intend to do. In the light of this knowledge, not using contraception is taking a risk if she knows her circumstances do not allow her to have a baby at that time. The risk includes both getting pregnant and having an abortion. Here I am mainly talking about women who do not use contraception, not about contraceptive failure.

'... All such examples have an unconscious meaning. Though the word unconscious is widely used in day-to-day speech, it is important to emphasise that it really means a person is completely unaware of their unconscious feelings, conflicts, meanings. The assumption I am making here is that many women who do not use contraception, or who use it incorrectly, do so for unconscious psychological reasons which include becoming pregnant and terminating the pregnancy. If you like, there is an element of "choice", i.e., a woman unconsciously "chooses" to become pregnant.

'I would like to state here that this concept of "choice" in a woman becoming pregnant could easily be used to blame women and abuse them in a way I strongly object to. My aim in introducing it is not to blame. On the contrary, I believe that through understanding the conflicts underlying her actions a woman can deal with these in a more direct way and be able to take responsibility for what she felt and what happened. Through this she can gain more control over her life and understand consciously the choices that she faces, thus not having to act out these conflicts in such a painful way as having an abortion or several abortions. In psychological terms, the more the unconscious can be made conscious, the more the woman is in control of her life.'

Conflicts that need to be made conscious may very often include those that stem from the image of femininity and motherhood in our society. When do we become 'real women'? Motherhood may be seen, unconsciously, as the most creative act available to women and yet there is a conflicting wish to be creative in a way other than having children. There may be a desire to be sexual but a fear of being sexual and confirmation, in an abortion, that being inappropriately sexual leads to negation of womanhood/motherhood.

These are deep waters indeed. Both Gillian and Mira will admit that, as analysts, their tendency is always to look beneath the given circumstances, such as contraceptive failure, to what may be behind an action or event. As Mira says: 'There are, of course, contraceptive failures. But sometimes there may be more to it than that. However I would not try to impose my understanding on anyone. I simply give women an opening to talk about these kinds of issues, to see if they have any echoes for them.'

Mira works with post-abortion therapy, where deeper motivations have more time to be explored and unfold. Pre-abortion counselling, usually lasting only 15 or 20 minutes, and even less or not at all in NHS hospitals, must have different aims. Depending upon the orientation of the counselling, the emphasis may be on medical grounds for abortion rather than on a woman's range of feelings, as Gillian explained above.

In her own pre-abortion counselling sessions, she has concentrated on encouraging women to feel freer to acknowledge their full range of feelings.

'Aborton is, literally, a loss and how people handle a loss is personal to them. It is part of growing. I would tell women that there is no *right* decision. Neither decision (to continue or to terminate the pregnancy) is painfree and, rather than get stuck in rightness and wrongness, they need to think in terms of the conditions they personally can best live with. They don't have to be perfect. Women often expect themselves to be superwoman and they need to realise that they can't be.

'I encourage women to talk as much as possible about their feelings to other people who are important to them — their partner, their family, their friends. But many, when I see them, have told no one. They feel ashamed and blameworthy and daren't tell anyone. I hope they feel a bit freer to talk after seeing me, once they have realised that I am not judgemental and therefore maybe certain others will not be either.'

Women's circumstances and attitudes towards an abortion may indicate whether they need help in coming to terms with it. 'I have never met a woman who used abortion as a form of contraception. Women who do have repeated abortions are in misery and conflict, inside themselves. If someone is doing something as painful as exposing herself to repeat abortions, I would try to help her discover what it is that she is trying to work out by doing it again and again. Or at least alert her to the fact that her actions are saying something which she may benefit from exploring, perhaps in therapy.

'A woman who feels nothing about having an abortion or the prospect of having an abortion is likely to be blocking some deep feelings about herself and motherhood. After all, even just the prospect of having an anaesthetic and surgery is usually in itself a bit frightening. Possibly she has fears about her ability to be a mother or a fear of being swamped by a baby. Whether she herself felt wanted as a baby may be an issue.'

She is not, however, saying that unless a woman feels terrible about having to have an abortion, she is suppressing a powder keg of potentially self-destructive feelings. 'When someone feels comfortable about abortion, she isn't necessarily cutting off her feelings. But she is someone who is able to live with a range of contradictory feelings. Or she may have had good support, been able to talk and to have had all the help she needed to go through it.'

One other helpful function of pre-abortion counselling can be to provide as much advance information as possible about the abortion procedure itself and what its effects may be.

'Research shows,' said Gillian, 'that the more you know (e.g., "You'll be taken into the waiting room first and have your notes taken, then you may have an hour to wait. You may feel cramps immediately after your operation. These may last for ..." etc.), the less fearful you are and the quicker you heal. Verbal information is better than written sheets which tend not to get read.

'On the emotional aspect of abortion, I have found that telling women beforehand that they *may* feel weepy, angry, sad, depressed, guilty, etc., for a while after the abortion, effectively gives them permission to *have* those feelings, if they come up, rather than suppress them. Very commonly women feel that, by choosing abortion, they have forfeited any right to those sorts of feelings.'

Many write to her afterwards to say that having the space to think without being judged and the permission to express their grief have been very important to them. 'Some choose to have one session afterwards, to make the event real and to cry and to place it in time and often that is enough,' she said.

Not that many women are lucky enough to get sensitive pre-abortion help of the kind Gillian offers. Mira started her post-abortion groups partly because pre-abortion counselling is so limited.

'But that is not the whole story,' she said. 'It is actually very upsetting having an abortion. It brings up a lot of feelings — pain, sadness, loss but also relief, hatred, anger, fear of sexuality or questions about one's femininity or sexuality. It is impossible to generalise about who will feel what or what the after-effects will be.'

Two that come up very often, she has found, tend to be around the issues of sex and babies.

'Suddenly you begin to notice babies or see friends with babies and it is painful,' she said. 'You may feel envious of women carrying babies and feel overwhelmed with a whole lot of feelings.

'After an abortion, some women become frightened that, if they have sex, they will get pregnant again and so come across as having lost interest in sex.'

'A woman may feel terribly invaded after an abortion,' said Gillian, 'and need privacy with her body for a while. Having felt so vulnerable over the abortion, she may need time before she can let herself feel vulnerable in sex again.

'Or she may not feel it is all right to have sex and be warm with someone unless children can be the result. This could have been the reason behind the unplanned pregnancy in the first place and then serve to put her off having sex afterwards.'

Abortion may make or break a relationship. 'For men, abortion can be very terrifying,' said Mira. 'It is a statement about a relationship that usually says, "I don't want your child" and that to him may be rejecting. The alternative, going through with a pregnancy, may seem to require a commitment that a man may find equally daunting. Men, being at one remove from abortion and because of conditioning against expressing feelings, often have even less chance than women to allow themselves to grieve.'

Some women may feel general relief and euphoria once the abortion is over and throw themselves into busy work and/or social lives. At this stage they do not feel any loss or guilt or other such feelings, and do not give themselves the space or time to feel them, but these may well surface much later and seem unconnected with the abortion. It is not uncommon, in Gillian and Mira's experience, for unfocused anxiety feelings, such as inability to sleep or concentrate at work, to start happening only a year or more after the abortion. Mira, in her chapter in *Living with the Sphinx* tells of a woman who saw a dead, featherless bird in a drain in her yard and ran back into the house and cried for hours, without knowing why she was doing so. Only after a few hours of crying did she realise that the bird without its feathers had looked like a foetus and triggered off the feelings she had suppressed since her abortion 20 years before.

Some women may appear to carry on their lives normally but feel detached and deadened, in an unconscious attempt to avoid feeling pain. Others may become extremely depressed about their lives and themselves, without relating that feeling directly to the abortion. They may consequently feel out of control and powerless generally.

There may be strong feelings of anger, directed against themselves or their partners or the hospital or clinic where they had the abortion. Or deep feelings of guilt and a sense of deserving punishment, a fitting one being an inability ever to have children. A very common fear is that permanent damage has been done by the abortion, especially if there has been a post-operative infection.

Whether women have had children before or not can have a bearing on their feelings. Mira said: 'Mothers tend to get more involved with what their child would have been like. They have living proof already of their child-bearing capacities and are seeing and enjoying one or more children grow up while they have prevented life for another. It may be a painful awareness. Conversely, they have the consolation that they do have children. The childless woman may often fear she will now never have the chance to have a baby.'

Gillian said: 'Some women with children do tend to feel more immediate guilt before an abortion. But others feel strongly that they already have the children they want and this decision is right for them.

'I think that, on the whole, however, the fantasy of what

it means to be a mother is in us from a very early age, regardless of whether one has had children or not. Some women who have never had children, and never wanted them, have a clear picture in their minds by six weeks of the baby they are carrying. Others never identify with what they are carrying and think of it as *an* embryo or *a* pregnancy. It all depends on the individual woman.'

Both agree that late abortion is an especially difficult experience, especially as a woman is often made to feel extremely guilty for not seeking help earlier.

'The women I saw who presented late tended to be young and come from countries where abortion is illegal or difficult,' said Gillian. 'Not all by any means looked pregnant. They were denying the pregnancy so much that finding they were over five months pregnant was a shock to everyone at examination. But however much they were denying, they were still feeling.'

Mira said: 'If women have to go through labour in late abortion, it is awful. It brings even more to the fore issues of life and death. Guilt is often confirmed by the attitude they meet from the medical profession. I do not feel punitive about late abortion. I think of it from the point of view of the mother who must have been going through so much for it to have got to that late stage at all.'

Some women have positive experiences of abortion, alongside the pain and sadness. Abortion may have been the first decision they have ever made alone in their lives; they may feel powerful to know they are fertile; they may have done something, for once, that they see as irresponsible, whereas normally they are practical and conscientious, and felt released by the experience.

This whole enormous pot-pourri of possible feelings, reactions and consequences can at least start to be explored, by those who choose to, in post-abortion counselling sessions or in post-abortion groups.

Mira's groups usually start with an evening session, followed by a whole day a week or so later. 'We dedicate the first evening to women talking to each other about their abortion — where, when, how they felt before and after. For some, it might be the first time they have ever spoken about their abortion. Everyone can get things off their chests while in a safe place — a group where others have all been through it too and so no one feels they are a freak for having their particular feelings.

'Some come a couple of days after an abortion, others come after 20 years. I try to pick up some threads of important issues, those areas that carry most energy for each particular woman — perhaps her relationship with her mother, her partner, her creativity, her work.

'I begin the whole day session by asking what has happened to people since they left the last group. Because, for many, it is quite an experience to have talked without being judged and a lot find they go and *do* something. For instance, one woman who hadn't had sex with her husband for years suddenly decided to have sex with him. One went to see the ex-boyfriend whom she had never before told that she had become pregnant by him and had had an abortion. For some women the first talk is not a big experience, but more usually it is. I am quite often surprised by the things they feel able to do, as a result of it.'

Much time is given to exploring, with support, any unconscious issues that led to pregnancy/abortion and need resolving. One woman at a group, for instance, didn't see her mother for six months after her abortion, whereas normally she was in very regular contact. She realised how suffocated she had felt by her mother and that the abortion was her way of going against her and saying 'get off my back'.

Whatever a woman's attitude towards herself and her abortion, there is the freedom to acknowledge it, without judgement from the group. Mira said: 'Abortion may be viewed as killing, as the removal of some cells or as the ending of a potential life. Whatever a woman's views, it is important that she can allow herself to say how she views it, rather than how she thinks she ought to view it.'

Similarly, she always points out to the group that, for some women, pregnancy starts as a very pleasant experience whereas others feel invaded by a monster. 'By saying this, I give room to women to say what *they* feel, not what they think they ought to feel.

'I do not impose my views. I only encourage women to think about the unconscious function of pregnancy/ abortion so that they don't have to repeat it.

'Talking about such things is, of course, just the beginning of an understanding. It creates a consciousness that there are certain things you need to work on in your life. My approach is try to take care of yourself. Be gentle. Try to make time for yourself, to write down what you think and feel. Lots of women are so busy in their lives that they don't get time to give in to what is going on for them.

'I do not believe that abortion is wrong. It comes out of much pain and conflict and brings much pain and conflict. If women have understood, from the group, what conflicts lay behind their pregnancy, then the abortion is also a positive for them, which brought the conflict into focus.

'Abortion is an indirect way of dealing with conflicting needs. A direct route needs to be found or, in some cases, an acceptance that a certain conflict can't be solved. We all have pains and losses in our lives that we have to bear. Acknowledgement makes them more bearable and lessens the need, unconsciously, to act them out painfully through perhaps pregnancy and abortion.'

8.
SEEKING
Useful information and addresses

Abortion laws vary from country to country and, in countries such as the United States and Australia, from state to state. The following is a rough guide, drawn from information contained in the last edition (1986) of *Induced Abortion: A World Review*, edited by Christopher Tietze and Stanley K. Henshaw. There may, however, have been changes since early 1986.

• *Abortion prohibited (or allowed only to save the life of the pregnant woman)*: Belgium, Ireland, Malta, most Muslim countries in Asia, two-thirds of Latin America and half of the countries of Africa.

• *Abortion permitted on wider medical grounds* (i.e., to avoid threat to a woman's health rather than specifically to her life and, sometimes, on grounds of genetic abnormality of the foetus or increased risk of abnormality): Canada, Spain, Portugal, South Africa.

• *Abortion permitted on medical and social grounds*: German Federal Republic, India, Japan, most of the socialist states of Eastern and Central Europe, Australia and the United Kingdom.

• *Abortion on request during first trimester and on medical grounds where necessary later*: Austria, China, Cuba, Denmark, France, German Democratic Republic, Italy, Netherlands, Norway, Singapore, Sweden, Tunisia, Turkey, United States, Soviet Union, Vietnam, Yugoslavia.

In different countries, medical and social grounds for abortion may have wide or narrow definitions but, in many, these are not strictly adhered to. Liberal laws, however, do not necessarily ensure easy availability. Lack of facilities or conservative attitudes among medical staff may limit access.

ADVICE SERVICES IN BRITAIN

Abortion Anonymous Counselling Service
Tel: 01-350 2229

A telephone help line, run by trained volunteers, for women who want to talk about their experience of abortion. The service is available from 7-9pm. Monday to Friday. Callers will hear a telephone answering message referring them to the correct number to ring that night. The above number for the message can be rung at any time during the day as well as the evening.

British Pregnancy Advisory Service (BPAS)
Austy Manor
Wootton Wowen
Solihull
West Midlands
Tel: 056 42 3225

A national non-profit making charity which provides information, pregnancy tests, pre- and post-abortion counselling and contraceptive advice. Branches in Basingstoke, Bath, Bedford, Birmingham, Bournemouth, Brighton, Cardiff, Chester, Coventry, Doncaster, Glasgow, Hull, Leamington Spa, Leeds, Liverpool, London, Luton, Manchester, Milton Keynes, Sheffield and Swindon. Where appropriate, abortions can be arranged at their nursing homes in Bournemouth, Brighton, Doncaster, Leamington Spa and Liverpool. Fees have to be charged.

Brook Advisory Centres
153a East Street
London SE17
Tel: 01-708 1234

50 Lower Gilmore Place
Edinburgh
Scotland SE17 25D
Tel: 031-229 3596
There are centres in London, Birmingham, Bristol,
Liverpool, Burnley, Coventry and Edinburgh, providing
pregnancy tests, pregnancy counselling, referral, post-
abortion counselling and general advice on sexual matters
and contraception for young women. The service is free bar
a small fee for pregnancy testing.

Care
790 Crookson Road
Glasgow G35 7TT
Tel: 041-882 6080
The Scottish Association for Care and Support after
Termination for Abnormality. A support group for parents
who face or have experienced a termination of pregnancy
after diagnosis of severe foetal abnormality or genetic
disease.

Family Planning Association
27-35 Mortimer Street
London W1N 7RJ
Tel: 01-636 7866

4 Clifton Street
Glasgow
Tel: 041-333 9696
Provides advice and information on family planning and
the addresses of local clinics

Marie Stopes House
108 Whitfield Street
London W1P 6BE
Tel: 01-388 2585/0662

Marie Stopes Centre
10 Queen Square
Leeds LS2 8AJ
Tel: (0532) 440685

Marie Stopes Centre

1 Police Street
Manchester M2 7LQ
Tel: 061-832 4260
The Marie Stopes Organization is a registered charity
concerned with women's health which provides pre- and
post-abortion counselling and, where appropriate,
arranges abortions at its clinics. Fee-charging.

New Grapevine

416 St John Street
London EC1V 4NJ
Tel: 01-278 9147
A counselling agency for young women, providing
individual post-abortion counselling, free by appointment,
for those in the Camden/Islington area; occasional post-
abortion workshops, free, for women in London; a
telephone helpline open to anyone and a drop-in service
for post-abortion counselling on Tuesdays between
10.30am and 2.30pm and Wednesday from 2.00pm till
6.30pm.

Pregnancy Advisory Service

11-13 Charlotte Street
London W1
Tel: 01-637 8962
Services include pre- and post-abortion counselling.
Abortion, where appropriate, can be arranged at their
clinic in Greater London. Fee-charging.

SAFTA

29-30 Soho Square
London W1V 6JB
Tel: 01-439 6124
Support after Termination for Abnormality, a support and
advice service for parents who face or have experienced
termination of pregnancy after diagnosis of foetal
abnormality.

The Women's Therapy Centre
6 Manor Gardens
London N7
Tel: 01-263 6200
Services include post-abortion counselling and groups.
Fee-charging.

Ulster Pregnancy Advisory Association
719a Lisburn Road
Belfast 9
Tel: Belfast (0232) 381345
Registered charity which offers pregnancy counselling and
arranges, where necessary, for assessment in England, as
abortion is illegal in Ireland. Post-abortion help available
too. Charges have to be made.

Women's Reproductive Rights Information Centre
52-4 Featherstone Street
London EC1Y 8RT
Tel: 01-251 6332
Provides information about all aspects of women's
reproductive health. Keeps lists, as far as possible, of post-
abortion groups in various parts of the country.

ABROAD

Women's Global Network on Reproductive Rights
PO Box 4098
1009 AB Amsterdam
Netherlands
Can provide advice, when available, on how to contact
groups or services which provide abortion help in other
countries.

ABOUT THE AUTHOR

DENISE WINN is a freelance writer and journalist specializing in medical and psychological topics.

A former editor of *Psychology Today* and of the magazine produced by MIND (National Association for Mental Health), she is the medical writer for *Cosmopolitan* and contributes regularly to other magazines and newspapers.

She has written several books including *The Hospice Way*, about the special quality of care offered by hospices to the terminally ill, and *Below the Belt*, a woman's guide to genito-urinary infections, both published by Optima.